ISBN- 978-0-9987735-9-9

ron@ronkarren.com
A division of AFP, Inc.

WHERE YOUR MONEY WENT AND HOW TO TAKE IT BACK

RONALD M. KARREN

TABLE OF CONTENTS

INTRODUCTION

WHAT YOU ARE ABOUT TO DISCOVER are tangible, viable solutions to two of the nation's most ominous and continually-growing crises:

- National and individual debt, and
- The failed retirement structures

Add to these the *projected-to-fail* Social Security system, and you have a recipe for the perfect financial catastrophe. The nation is long overdue for solutions that rebuild and bolster our vital middle class.

The solutions to these two most critical issues are found in two specific formulations, each independent, yet complimentary, to each other. These formulations are:

- New Debt-Acceleration Formulations, and
- Deferred Income Accounts (as opposed to *Deferred Tax Accounts*—401(k), IRA, 403(b), etc.)

As you will discover, these two formulations are highly impactful, life-changing, and applicable to everyone regardless of where they fall on the economic spectrum. These formulations, with their strategies and protocols, benefit individuals, homeowners, banks, and investment administrators equally—a veritable win/win/win scenario.

For nearly two decades, I have researched, hypothesized, discussed, and debated these concepts with some of the nation's leading financial experts along with CEOs, CPAs, bankers, lawyers, investment brokers, employee-benefits administrators, real estate brokers, and insurance brokers, many of whom became clients.

Through these decades of market testing, my clients have paid their homes off in an average of 8 years and 11 months, as opposed to 26 years and 9 months, the average life of the mortgages (combined with their consumer debts).

This reduction in mortgage time has created a saving of $164,000 per household in mortgage and consumer-debt interest. This savings was realized by simply changing their daily banking behaviors and following basic concepts: a set of financial concepts of which very few CPAs or financial professionals have a full understanding.

As for the investment/retirement formulations, these clients have shifted their investment strategies from the losing propositions of the failed *pension structure* and/or from the failed *Pre-Tax Structure* (e.g. the 401(k), IRA, 403(b), etc.), and into new, innovative investment vehicles that are neither subject to market loss nor to taxes when configured properly.

These have the added safety features of:

- Highly-regulated reserve rates ten times higher than that of banks
- Multi-tiered regulatory oversight; and,
- A legally-binding contract that governs performance of the account

Upon removing the factors of market loss and taxes, and when considering the entire life of these investment vehicles (e.g. from the funding phase, through the disbursement phase, and the final settlement phase upon the account-holder's death), these investment vehicles can typically outperform the traditional investment vehicles by a factor of ten. When combining these two formulations, no other approach on the market competes with this level of savings, production, and safety, wherein all parties win.

With this quantifiable data now proven over the past two decades, the debate is over. It is time to change paradigms, protocols, and practices. This can be done one way: through education of the masses. This book is the key. When you are finished reading it, share it.

ACKNOWLEDGEMENTS

THIS WORK REALLY BELONGS TO MANY INDIVIDUALS with whom I have sat, supped, configured and conversed on seemingly endless financial topics. Hence, both this book and the collection of financial concepts have come together, piece by piece, over time. More notably, it all came together about the same time as the period of the Great Recession

The fact that these mathematical seedlings both took root and flourished beyond expectation, especially during the most financially turbulent era known to the last three generations of Americans, speaks to their viability, effectiveness, as well as to their immunity to deep market corrections. In fact, the retirement configuration (called the *Deferred Income Account*) actually thrived during these volatile-markets.

Thanks to each and all of you confidants and clients for your sounding-board services, your participation in thinking through and eventually implementing these concepts. This process has not only *enabled* me, but it has also *pushed* me to continually vet and prove each of these concepts and formulation before taking them to market.

With the assistance of great staff members, these concepts have materialized into well-thought-out, organized protocols that correlate chronologically with life's financial stages, namely: credit and credit-related issues of early adulthood; mortgage, asset protection, tax strategies for the middle aged; and viable retirement strategies for everyone.

Also, a special thanks to the National Association of State Boards of Accountancy (NASBA) for having an open mind to new ideas, and then both assessing and certifying these concepts for CPA continued-education. A resounding thank-you to you CPAs and accountants as well, for not only offering your valuable assistance and insights for honing these formulations, but also for sharing them with your clients!

Lastly, this book is dedicated to my 1,000+ clients who, through their trust, put their personal finances and investment strategies on the line sufficiently to allow me to prove the effectiveness of these formulations, and did so during one of the most chaotic economic eras in U.S. history. That is trust! Thanks to each of you!

CHAPTER 1

Redistribution of Wealth vs. Reconsolidation of Wealth (And Its Relevance to You)

TO UNDERSTAND WHERE *YOU* ARE FINANCIALLY, in terms of how the larger economic construct is affecting your finances, earning ability, the actual worth of your money, etc., it is crucial to understand where we are as a nation *financially*. This is for the fact that your financial health, or financial opportunity, for the most part is dependent on the nation's financial health. For example, if money is pooled and scarce, much like it was throughout the recent decade of recession, it is most likely going to have an impact on you as a wage earner, a consumer, an investor, a business owner, and even as a voter.

With this knowledge, we can not only avoid the errors of past generations, but we can learn from their mistakes and form better strategies in finance, and increase the investment odds for retirement and retirees in the investment realm.

THE ORIGINAL DISTRIBUTION AND RECONSOLIDATION OF WEALTH

Since the dawn of civilization, and particularly since record keeping, the wealth of the world has been amassed and controlled by the ruling classes or monarchies. With the overthrow and replacement of the world's monarchies, and with the advent of the United States, members of these monarchies brought their wealth to invest in the new American experiment, therein still maintaining a massive divide in terms of wealth distribution.

With few exceptions, up until 1930 the world never experienced a true distribution of wealth. Even at that point in time, the disparity of income, or the level of wealth consolidation "at the very top," was such that the top 10% of the wealthiest individuals were taking 50% of the national income.

This income disparity was a result of these top ten-percenters having a head start, so to speak, with the massive funds from the dismantled monarchies, which archaic structure transitioned into oligarchies. Depending on your political lenses, these oligarchies maintained their power, transitioned their power, or perhaps, established their "new power" by creating monopolies in railroads, oil and gas, chemical, and other industries. As history shows, these power brokers wielded their power aggressively upon their laborers, and upon the consumers—the very nature of *monopoly*.

In time, the U.S. began the first and largest *Distribution of Wealth* in history. It was a crucial, world-changing event.

In the post-Depression era of the 1930s, the masses began to form unions, therein influencing the politics and legislation of the country. To level the playing field with the oligarchies and the other nouveau-riches of the world, anti-trust laws were enacted to keep these top 10-percenters from establishing these monopolies, or from snuffing out their competitive upstarts. To name a few of the improvements, sweeping legislation removed children from mines and unsafe factories, improved unhealthy working conditions and hours, and shut down the enslaving company-store concept. The anti-trust (anti-monopoly) legislation enabled entrepreneurs and upstarts to enter the marketplace, creating the necessary competition to drive prices down for consumers, therein opening the door for what would become the greatest middle class in U.S. history, and perhaps, in the history of mankind.

With the uniting of the masses who pushed for wealth redistribution, by 1950 the U.S.:

- Established the largest middle class on earth
- Became the most politically stable democracy, and
- Became a World Power with the largest, most-productive economy on the planet.

The basic premise of a stable society and government, as taught in beginning economics or political science courses, is a large, productive middle class. As a result, the most notable indicator of success of this era is measured in the following statistic:

> *In the 1950s, the top 10% of the wealthiest individuals were now taking only 10% of the national income (as opposed to 50% in 1930).*

In those few decades, an additional 40% of the nation's income had been redirected to the masses, resulting in the most significant distribution of wealth in history.

Fast forward five decades to 2008: after two back-to-back recessions, jobless recoveries, and extreme losses in retirement accounts (401(k)s, IRAs, and other *pre-tax* vehicles), the United States was facing the same pre-Depression wealth-consolidation statistics. By 2008, the wealthiest 10% were once again taking 50% of the national income—with some data indicating a 52% to 55% share.

The great Distribution of Wealth of 1930-1950 had been erased, and with it went the productive, consuming, and politically-stabilizing middle class.

> [Side Bar: Through this first and very successful Distribution of Wealth, we learned that when a nation's wealth is consolidated in large pools, controlled by few, a nation will stagnate for the simple fact that the economy will stagnate. Putting this in very simple terms: When a nation's wealth is consolidated into the accounts of a few billionaires, the billionaires can feasibly purchase and maintain a small number of mansions or yachts throughout his or her life.

These large but few purchases do not create enough jobs for mansion contractors or yacht builders, when compared to a scenario where these billions of dollars are spread over a few thousand people who would require the construction of 1000 homes, 500 apartments, and 750 automobiles—therein truly stimulating the economy, where the masses and the economy benefit.

When it is the middle class who has an equal distribution or equal portion of money, it does not stagnate in centralized or elitist pools. Stagnant pools of money promote a stagnant economy. When the middle class experiences an equal flow of funds, it not only creates businesses, it also actively engages in spending the money for travel, hobbies, eating out, buying gifts (i.e. dispersing it in ALL directions, which enables entrepreneurial and technological innovations and progression, and myriad other benefits).

Most importantly, a thriving, healthy, and robust middle class serves as a stabilizing factor in the economy, thereby helping the Federal Reserve and the government itself to avoid large financial crises. Simultaneously, it safeguards against, or lessens the impact of, large-scale scandals on the economy.]

Since the Great Recession spanning from 2001 to 2008, the subject of wealth redistribution has taken center stage, with accolades from the political left; and, generally, with hisses and boos from the right.

However, the great divide between these parties is not centered in the importance or the need for a redistribution of wealth (as even conservatives believe in the great middle-class concept). The pivotal issue of wealth redistribution is how to bring about a fair and equitable redistribution of wealth without engaging in the divisive *take-from-the-rich-and-give-to-the-poor* methodologies, or by means of needless taxation, or by social-justice measures. If a viable redistribution can be executed without further taxation or government intervention (i.e. by free-market forces). And if it can be done quickly and efficiently for the sake of the middle class and the poor, all the better!

There are several models to bring about the needful redistribution of wealth fairly and equitably. I have found two of these models in two distinct financial industries, which could bring about a redistribution of wealth far greater than the 1930's Original Distribution—doing so in half the time, having twice the impact, wherein all parties win: the consumers, the banks, Corporate America, and ultimately, the economy as a whole. After all, a stable and robust economy benefits everyone. And yes, this also includes the poor, as a stable and robust economy provides more opportunity for upward mobility, as well as increased funding for those agencies engaged in assisting those facing challenges during their upward mobility.

The pathway to this mutually-beneficial, economy-stabilizing solution is found in both the *Debt-Finance* and *Retirement-Finance* industries.

In these past two decades, I have developed a working model that brings about an extremely efficient, effective, as well as a fair and equitable redistribution of wealth. When applying the proven results of these models to a macro-economic scale, the results are exciting. As to the fair and equitable attributes of this redistributive model, the redistribution is accomplished through free-market forces with simple over-the-counter banking products, and by simply changing a few of your daily, weekly, or monthly banking behaviors.

On the retirement-finance side of the model, it simply requires a common-sense assessment of the current retirement systems: take the good aspects, reject the failed aspects, and then simply opt for the better system.

Before explaining details of these proven models however, we must return and finish our history lesson. This is necessary because it is in our history that we find many of the answers on how to effectively bring about this redistribution of wealth in a fair and equitable manner for all.

With income-disparity ratios of 2008 coming full circle by mirroring the income-disparity ratios of 1929, the questions before us are: *how* and *when* was this Pre-1950s Great Redistribution of Wealth reversed? What happened, and why?

THE GREAT RECONSOLIDATION OF WEALTH

Starting in the early 1970s, there was big push to centralize everything. To further the aims of the already established Central Bank, President Nixon officially took us off the Bretton Woods system (successor to the Gold Standard), taking us into the new economic era of the Fiat Economy. Thereafter, the value of the U.S. dollar was no longer tied to gold, nor by a "promise" to back the holder of a Treasury Note with gold. Instead, the value of the dollar was established by *fiat*, or decree, by the government, or Federal Treasury.

Moreover, and more destructively, from the Nixon Administration came the campaign of *Get Big or Get Out*. Under Nixon's Secretary of Agriculture, Earl Butz, this campaign was the start of both the consolidation and centralization of the food supply, driving independent farmers out of business. At the height of this nationwide campaign to consolidate land, food supply, and the revenue therefrom, celebrities, like Bruce Springsteen and Willie Nelson, were hosting concerts and events such as FarmAid, to lessen the plight of independent farmers, or save them from bankruptcy.

Hollywood mobilized to create films on this topic such as *Country* (Jessica Lang), *The River* (Sissy Spacek), and others. It was a national crisis that no one could deter, and the decimation of our independent agricultural producers (i.e. our middle class) had swung into high gear. Where independent farmers, butchers, and bakers dotted our countryside and Main Streets, they have been replaced by a literal handful of mega-corporations. Not only was the revenue of our food supply reconsolidated back to the top power brokers, but the ultimate control of the food supply itself had been consolidated into the hands of the power brokers.

Deregulation, or lack of regulation, gave these mega-corporations a tremendous advantage, and has become a crucial element in the destruction of the middle class, especially when it comes to finance. In the financial sector, there has been an egregious lack of regulation, as evidenced by the continual loss of investments, pensions, and retirements due to Wall Street ineptness and corruption.

This lack of regulation in the financial sector is largely due to the influence of one man: The Wizard of Wall Street.

Alan Greenspan stepped into the national spotlight in 1976 under President Ford and has served as the lead financial expert, the Presidents' go-to guy from Ford to Obama, and the ultimate financial "guru." At his swearing-in ceremony in the Oval Office with the Fords, Greenspan invited his idol and inspiration Ayn Rand, an ultra-conservative, laissez-faire author and ideologue.

The theme of governance in those decades truly became laissez-faire: "go with the flow", the markets will work themselves out naturally, the system will weed out frauds, cheaters, scams, and will eventually correct itself. Unfortunately, this doesn't work for retirees. For them, there are no second chances to go back in time and start funding their retirements all over again. Eventual Correction doctrine of this laissez-faire wizard does not work for this demographic.

Due to rampant fraud on Wall Street, by the mid-1990s these losses of billions of retirement dollars were literally putting elderly people on the streets. In the face of such massive destruction, someone had to pick up the tab immediately because of the immediacy of lost retirement funds (i.e. immediate homelessness for many). The taxpayer was the only group capable of paying the tab for these rampant banker scams and broker frauds that the laissez-faire doctrine never weeded out. Today, the tax-payers are still on the hook because regulation is still far too ineffective. As bankers and brokers know this, they continue lobbying against balanced legislation and regulation.

[Side Bar: To understand the win-lose nature of Wall Street investing, especially where retirement accounts are concerned, it helps to realize three basic premises:

1. Placing your dollar bills on the stock market is no different than placing a bet. A Wall Street transaction is a mere and sheer gamble.

2. Dollars on the stock market are finite, meaning there is only a limited number of them. Because dollars are finite, all Wall Street players (brokers, hedge fund managers, companies, and various indexes themselves) are competing for those dollars to be "bet" on them and/or their stock picks.

3. Because dollars are finite, when someone wins, someone else loses. Therefore, if someone unfairly wins by cheating, fraud, insider-trading, etc., then someone loses unfairly, for the fact that those finite dollars went to the cheaters.

4. When the winners have an advantage, the losers' odds of gaining decrease. Where consumers are conditioned that Wall Street investing requires a "long-term" strategy; with super computers now employed by the big banks and brokers, the average time that a stock is held, meaning the time that it is bought and then sold, was only 22 seconds as of 2016. This is

where the big money is being made; wherein these financial houses are purchasing millions of shares, and when that stock increases by one cent ($0.01) two seconds after the purchase, their super computer sells it back off, making that firm $10,000 in 2 seconds.]

With these preceding concepts in mind, consider where your retirement dollars are, and how they are supposedly competing fairly on what is supposed to be a level playing field. To further expose the unlevel nature of this playing field, also consider the following list of indictments over a three-year period. Pay close attention to dollar amounts, and particularly to the amounts made versus the fines paid for cheating. Notice who the perpetrators are (whose names I have emphasized in bold).

2003 MUTUAL FUND SCANDAL

1. *On April 28, 2003, every major US investment bank, including Merrill Lynch, Goldman Sachs, Morgan Stanley, Citigroup, Credit Suisse, First Boston, Lehman Brothers Holdings, J.P. Morgan Chase, UBS Warburg, and U.S. Bancorp Piper Jaffray, were found to have aided and abetted efforts to defraud investors. The firms were fined a total of $1.4 billion by the SEC, triggering the creation of a Global Research Analyst Settlement Fund.*

2. *In May, 2003, the SEC disclosed that several "brokerage firms paid rivals that agreed to publish positive reports on companies whose shares they issued to the public. This practice made it appear that a throng of believers were recommending these companies' shares." This was false. "From 1999 through 2001, for example, one firm paid about $2.7 million to approximately 25 other investment banks for these so-called research guarantees, regulators said. Nevertheless, the same firm boasted in its annual report to shareholders that it had come through investigations of analyst conflicts of interest with its 'reputation for integrity' maintained."*

3. *On September 3, 2003, the New York State Attorney General announced he had "obtained evidence of widespread illegal trading schemes, 'late trading' and 'market timing,' that potentially cost mutual fund shareholders billions of dollars annually." This, according to the Attorney General, was "no different than betting on a horse race after the horses have crossed the finish line."*

4. *On September 4, 2003, a major investment bank,* ***Goldman Sachs****, admitted that it had violated anti-fraud laws. Specifically, the firm misused material, nonpublic information that the US Treasury would suspend issuance of the 30-year bond. The firm agreed to "pay*

over $9.3 million in penalties." On April 28, 2003, the same firm was found to have "issued research reports that were not based on principles of fair dealing and good faith... contained exaggerated or unwarranted claims...and/or contained opinions for which there were no reasonable bases." The firm was fined $110 million dollars, for a total of $119.3 million dollars in fines in six months.

5. *On November 20, 2003, the Securities and Exchange Commission announced "charges concerning undisclosed market timing against Harold J.* ***Baxter*** *and Gary L.* ***Pilgrim*** *in the Commissions' pending action in federal district court in Philadelphia." In a later settlement, Baxter and Pilgrim agreed to "pay $80 million – $60 million in disgorgement and $20 million in civil penalties."*

This three-year list contains the indictments carried out by New York's Attorney General Elliot Spitzer. This list contains another 35 entries which run through 2006. Though it is not clear who compiled the actual list, this public information has been reported by various reporting entities. Each act is verifiable, and the list can be obtained by searching the phrase "2003 Mutual Fund Scandal". Therein you will find familiar names like Tyson Foods, Citigroup, Kmart, and McAfee along with the top Wall Street banks, bankers, and brokers. I used this three-year data set for the fact that all this corruption, which lost trillions of American's retirement dollars, was known to Alan Greenspan who had previously slapped the label of *irrational exuberance* on the Wall Street Bankers in his speech at the American Enterprise Institution on Dec. 5, 1996. It was absurd for him to step forward on October 23, 2008, *after* trillions of retirement dollars were lost, and claim to Congress: "My views of how the world worked were flawed." He knew what was going on the entire time, and his views were no more flawed in 2008 than they were 12 years earlier in 1996. As I will touch on momentarily, it was Greenspan who was key in persuading President Bill Clinton to shut down Brooksley Born's efforts to have the destructive derivatives regulated.

This is neither the make-up of a prodigy child nor a proclaimed "Financial Wizard." This is a frail old man hiding behind a curtain with a loud-speaker; all smoke and mirrors. Whether intentional or otherwise, he paved the way for Wall Street corruption to perpetually thrive throughout his tenure.

[Side Bar: The vehicle largely responsible for the loss of wealth in the U.S. during Greenspan's reign was the *derivative*. Here is the definition of a derivative according to the Office of the Comptroller of the Currency, U.S. Department of Treasury (retrieved Feb. 2013):

> *A derivative is a financial* ***contract*** *whose value is derived from the performance of underlying market*

factors, such as interest rates, currency exchange rates, and commodity, credit, and equity prices.

Derivative Transactions include an assortment of financial contracts, including structured debt obligations and deposits, swaps, futures, options, caps, floors, collars, forwards, and various combinations thereof.

In essence, a derivative is a contractual bet or wager formed by two or more entities that is based on whatever factors on which they want to bet. It is the ultimate vice for high-stakes gambling addicts, such as Greenspan's irrationally exuberant big bankers and Wall Street high rollers. This presents two disturbing problems:

1. These addicts aren't gambling with *their* money: All too often, these unregulated bets include massive blocks of retirement funds or pension funds; and/or assets that exceed these addicts' ability to pay.

2. Because derivatives are simply bets in the form of a contract, no governing agency can monitor them, as they are not stocks or securities. They are not registered anywhere, since they are simply enforceable "bets" in the form of a **contract**. These contracts sit where most contracts sit: in the private safes of private citizens, private entities, or

private law firms. Therefore, only the gambling addicts and their attorneys know what is really at risk.

Item two (above) is what caused so much consternation during the 2008 crash, when the remedial decisions had to be made by government: *Which firms do we bail out, and which firms do we let fail?* With the first failures in the 2008 crash (Bear Stearns and Lehman Brothers), the government learned just how destructive derivatives were.

Generally and briefly, after months of calculations and arriving at the amount of $30B (or so) to save Bear Stearns, and after the deal was struck, Bear Stearns stepped forward with, "Oh, by the way…our attorneys have now divulged the *other* contractual bets [derivatives] we made, which are in their safes. They include our *losing derivatives* [contracts] for which we are also *legally* liable; therefore, we need to restructure the bailout package to include an additional $15B [or so]." When it came time to deal with Lehman Brothers, the government was now "on to" the true nature of derivatives, so they let Lehman Bros. fail. The Obama administration was highly criticized for "picking and choosing" whom it bailed out and whom it did not.

More disturbing is the fact the Clinton Administration had the window of opportunity to get derivatives regulated, but chose not to. In 1996, President Bill Clinton appointed attorney

Brooksley Born, a Stanford University law graduate as the Chair to the Commodity Futures Trading Commission (CFTC). There, she recognized the dire need to begin regulating these unregulated bets. To do so, she had to go up against The Great Wizard of Wall Street (Alan Greenspan), smitten in his affair with Ayn Rand's laissez-faire economics.

In short, Greenspan circled the wagons consisting of Robert Rubin, Arthur Levitt, Lawrence Sumners, Timothy Geithner, and most importantly, President Bill Clinton, to shut down Ms. Born's efforts. She was forced to resign by 1999. Within two years, the first ripple of losses from derivatives shocked the markets, sparked by overvalued companies and IPOs. This was exacerbated by the 911 attacks, then further exacerbated by the Enron-Arthur Anderson scandal. The ensuing derivative wave hit the market in 2008 wherein we truly witnessed firsthand the devastation caused by derivatives, as explained earlier with the Lehman Brothers example. Though President Clinton is often found gloating in the economic results of the 1990s new-tech rise, in reality he chose Greenspan over Ms. Born, thus allowing derivatives to continue unregulated. Had he acted on Born's recommendation, we might have averted one of the two great recessions, or, at minimum, lessened the impact or severity of them both.

To date, all of Greenspan's cronies who condemned Ms. Born, and stopped her attempts to reign in the practices of our irrationally-exuberant gambling addicts, have completely changed their position and opinions on derivatives. They are now calling for regulation just as Ms. Born had done two decades earlier. Are derivatives regulated yet? *No!* And for this, we can expressly thank Alan Greenspan, Nixon, Ford, Reagan, Bush I & II, and Obama. But President Clinton is personally responsible for shutting down Ms. Born, the *one person* who saw the danger, waved the flags, and who boldly set out to correct it.

Most analysts agree that the aggregated value of derivatives was estimated to be at about $1.2 quadrillion as of 2013—about 5 times the amount of actual money in the world (which is only about $200 trillion).]

That said, with this supreme Wizard of Wall Street who served as the financial go-to guy for at least six presidents over the past 40 years, the very Wizard who shut down the efforts of Brooksley Born to regulate the highly destructive derivative gambling table at the infamous Wall Street Casino, the very Wizard who claimed his views were flawed, whose previous statements showed that he was acutely aware of the gambling addicts' vices, we must ask ourselves:

Is our monetary policy and its governing heads really that shallow, fragile, and misguided?

Now the question for the U.S. citizenry is: *Can we bring about a fair and equitable redistribution of wealth, and can it be done expeditiously in order to save our middle class, and not risk ANY segment of the economy?* To this I offer a resounding *Yes!* The models are in place. The testing has been done with hundreds of clients, and the results are in. All that is necessary are open minds (and ears), and eighth-grade level math skills. These two revolutionary approaches to *Debt-Finance* and *Retirement-Finance* work for everyone equitably, regardless of their position on the economic spectrum.

It would certainly speed things up if local banks and/or credit unions caught the vision of this, and began structuring accounts that would bring this change about more effectively, as there are ways to minimize *all* risk on their part. However, banks are typically slow to evolve, despite our ability to quantify immediate and substantive profits for them. And yet even with their current archaic and often illogical over-the-counter banking products, we can still achieve the desired results, just as we have been doing here in the U.S. for the past two decades.

[Side Bar: Companies can also assist in bringing this change about immediately and most effectively as detailed in the last chapter of this book. For employers struggling with the 401(k) concept, Chapter 7 is a must read. For employees or the self-employed who need to improve the odds and the production of their retirement accounts, Chapters 5 and 6 will prove most beneficial.]

CHAPTER 2

The Rise of Accelerated-Mortgage Banking

IN EARLY 2002, I WAS APPROACHED by the firm *Everyday Wealth* of Austin, TX. *Everyday Wealth was* a joint venture between three of the nation's leading CEOs, including Bill Fields of Walmart Stores. Their goal was to get Americans out of debt faster in the aftermath of the 2001 economic crash.

The reason behind this effort was that prior to 2001, Walmart was experiencing an approximate 12% share of the discretionary income per household. After the three-year economic downturn, their share of America's discretionary income was cut in half to 6%. Instead of spending, Americans were focused on reducing their debts.

Their specific approach was based on the traditional concepts as taught by the nation's leading gurus who had been teaching the same thing for 100 years (i.e. *pay off your highest-interest debt first, increase your credit score so that you can qualify for better interest loans,* and *tighten your belt in order to save sufficient money to pay off the next debt,* etc.).

Everyday Wealth specifically sought out my technological, scriptwriting, and production services to create their educational and marketing productions. It was in the scriptwriting phase that I saw the inherent flaws of their concepts and overall approach. During the production process, I was also introduced to the mortgage finance concepts from Australia. At first I was skeptical, but in the ensuing days, weeks, and months, it became an all-consuming subject for me. It was so simple, yet so revolutionary in terms of bringing about impactful changes in several financial industries, especially when compared to the archaic concepts being taught in the educational production, which I was directing.

After the first few weeks of studying the concepts, I pitched the ideas to the *Everyday Wealth* team. However, their gurus had no interest in it. Within the ensuing years, *Everyday Wealth* closed its doors, and the Australian concept continued to grow in popularity nationwide. Additionally, the nation's renown financial gurus began denouncing the new Australian-banking concepts on their syndicated financial programs, claiming they "ran the numbers and it just doesn't add up."

Simultaneous to their statements denouncing these consumer-geared concepts, I was presenting a very different message to the frontline finance professionals around the country:

> *With basic 8th-grade math skills (addition, subtraction, multiplication, and division), one can easily validate the veracity and effectiveness of the Australian-banking concepts.*

When put into a spreadsheet, it is a mathematical cakewalk. What the establishment professionals have failed to identify are the nuances of behavior and subsequent paradigm shifts that take place because of the new mathematical formulations and new knowledge. The resulting exponential savings on debt-interest savings are irrefutable. The macroeconomic prospects (i.e. wealth redistribution): revolutionary!

All that these "gurus" had to do was look at the math *and* take note of the behavioral changes of these client-consumers. Today, these "financial experts" no longer need to rely on simple *math theory*. We now have the actual client files proving the reality of its effectiveness—all verifiable with 8th-grade math skills.

Originally, there were just two companies offering the service. Having dealt with both firms, I discovered flaws in their math, and therefore their overly-optimistic projections. With no response to my calls to correct their math, I set out to construct a math engine that could accurately account for both *interest-only* and *fixed-rate* mortgages, a gaping flaw in their structures. Eighteen months later, the math engine was proven accurate and market-ready—again, with basic math skills.

Within weeks of completing the math engine, I was approached by the brother of a Utah governor, who ran a large financial planning firm in Layton, Utah. After a lengthy presentation to him in my office, he invited me to his offices to present to their staff and various associates comprised of attorneys, bankers, CPAs, real estate brokers, investment brokers, insurance brokers, etc. What was planned as a 90-minute meeting, turned into an all-day affair as I stood at the whiteboard writing out the concepts, the math, and fielding a barrage of questions.

At the end of the day, with no substantive rebuttals or surviving arguments, I realized the significant value of these formulations and concepts. My first clients came from this group of professionals.

At the time, the fledgling industry was known as *Australian Mortgage*, as this entire approach was (and still is) literally based on the way mortgages are structured in Australia. Though many service providers sprang from the original importers of the concept, very few of these service providers have survived, especially after 2008. I attribute this to many factors including a broad misunderstanding of the tool, poor consumer applications, and poor business models.

What is important at this point is *how* this landmark concept all came about in Australia, and how it relates not only to the U.S. economy and the middle class, but also to *you* as an individual consumer. For this, we need another short history lesson. Pay close attention, because this history lesson isn't simply for the sake of remembering. There are crucial concepts in this lesson that apply directly to you *if* you are interested in paying off your mortgage and/or consumer debt <u>in one-third the time, saving two-thirds the interest</u>, as well as interested in saving our middle class.

[Side Bar: If the middle class continues its decline, the economy will suffer tremendously as explained in a previous Side Bar in Chapter 1. The reality of obtaining property or a home will become an extreme rarity. If we lose the middle class, we lose this country as we know it. The masses will, once again, be controlled by the elite few, who now control the three

M's: Money, Manna, and Military, just as it has through the eons of empires, monarchies, communism, dictatorships, and oligarchies. Democracy is commensurate to the size of its middle class. The greater the middle class, the greater and more stable the democracy.]

Though it is not crucial to know the exact history of this lesson, as it has no bearing on the net results of the mortgage or debt acceleration concepts, it is interesting to see this banking evolution and its relevance to debt/mortgage acceleration.

THE S&L CRISIS AND THE LESSONS LEARNED

Between 1980 and 1990, Federal Savings and Loans (S&Ls) failed, which reasons ranged from poor loan-to-holdings ratios to high-risk investing, and lack of oversight. As a remedy to the massive failure, the S&L industry was merged with traditional banking institutions, while the Federal Saving & Loan Insurance Corporation (FSLIC) was merged with the Federal Deposit Insurance Corporation (FDIC), the entity that *insures* (and I use this term very liberally) your bank deposits.

Long story short: the U.S. Congress revised the reserve requirements to ensure that Americans would not lose their bank deposits. To date, Federal Reserve levels are about ten cents on reserve for every dollar you have deposited into *smaller* banks, whereas *large* banks are generally not required to have any reserves. The average reserve requirement is about six cents for every dollar you have in your savings, checking, or certificate of deposit (CD) accounts.

What became paramount in this corrective restructuring of the U.S. banking system was this: banks were prohibited from taking $0.94 cents of every dollar, and directly investing it for the bank's gain. Instead, banks had to qualify for lines of credit with either a larger bank, or with the Fed. If/When investments failed, the bank itself would be responsible for the losses first through its lines of credit, and then with its pledged assets that backed those lines of credit.

Additionally, with a balance on their line of credit (LOC) these banks would also have to pay Daily Calculated Interest (DCI), interest that is calculated daily, seven days per week, 365 days per year.

However, to ease their burden of this DCI, the Fed allowed the banks a tremendous "out" from having to pay the DCI: they could take all the monies deposited into their cash accounts (i.e. checking, saving, certificate of deposit, et al) up to the federal reserve limits of the 94% average, and deposit that cash into their lines of credit, saving massive amounts of interest expense.

Example: let's say that ABC Bank established their LOC with a larger bank, and they took $100K from their newly-established LOC to invest in widgets, wherein they were earning a 15% return. Simultaneously, because this money was pulled from their LOC, they were being charged DCI at 2%. This means that every day, they were charged $5.48 for this loan ($164.38/month).

Let's say that the depositors of ABC Bank had a cumulative amount of $100K in their cash accounts (from their customers' deposits); and, ABC Bank also had a reserve limit of $0.06, or 6%. This would mean that ABC Bank could take 94% of the $100K deposits (or $94,000) and move that "cash" to their LOC, where it sits against *their* debt.

This maneuver immediately reduced the balance of their $100K line of credit, down to $6,000. Therefore, their DCI on the following day would only be assessed on that $6,000 balance. Because they are able to take 94% of their customers' cash deposits (or $94,000 out of the $100K customer deposits) and apply that money to their $100K debt in their LOC, the bank would be charged $0.33 per day (2% annual interest on $6000) rather than the $5.48 per day (2% annual interest rate for the $100K). That is 16 times less!

U.S. BANKER LINE OF CREDIT TEMPLATE

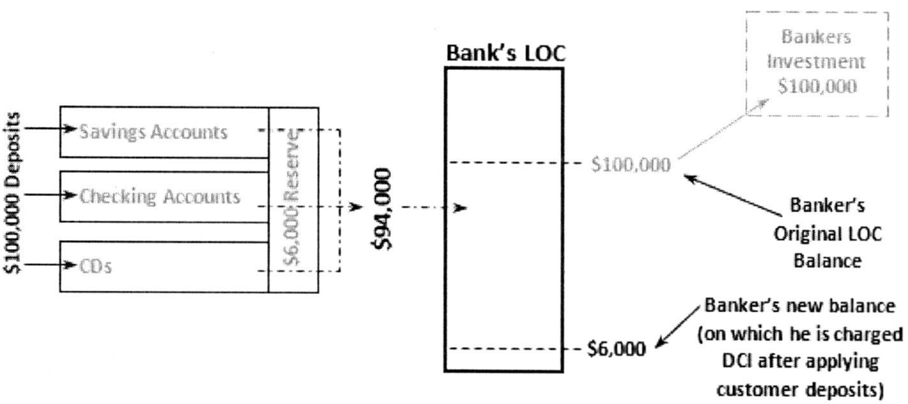

This mirrors the Australian banking system. Within this system, Australian mortgages operate in the identical manner in which lines of credit operate for the banks—each reaping huge benefits where this protocol is in practice. That said, let's restructure the math to illustrate exactly how it works for Australians.

THE AUSTRALIAN MORTGAGE STRUCTURE

In Australia, mortgages are structured much like an *open line of credit* (LOC). Because the mortgage has the same characteristics as a LOC, Australians can put as much money against their mortgage as they wish, with the option of pulling that money out at any time, as they want or need it. This very simple option is crucial to paying off not just your mortgage in one third the time, but also paying off *any* debt in one-third the time, and therein saving, or retaining, two thirds the interest.

Let's take an average Australian income of $80,000/year, and strap this homeowner with a $195,000 mortgage; and, to keep numbers simple, let's say the *net* take-home pay (after taxes, health insurances, etc.) is $5,000 per month.

> [Side Bar: For the bank's protection, they typically set a borrowing limit at about the 80% Loan-to-Value mark for HELOCs. This means that the homeowner in this example would have a market value on his home of $275,000, with loan limit up to the $220,000 mark (80% of $275,000). In that there is already a mortgage balance of $195,000, this would mean that this homeowner would have access of about $25,000 of that amount (i.e. the $220,000 limit minus the mortgage balance of $195,000 = $25,000 accessible funds).]

When the $5,000 paycheck comes in for our Australian homeowner [let's call him Joey, for expediency] his money does not sit in his checking or savings account. Instead, his $5,000 is deposited directly into his mortgage, thereby reducing the mortgage balance down from $195,000 to $190,000. With this deposit, Joey is now assessed DCI on $190,000, rather than on the previous day's balance of $195,000.

For every day that Joey's entire paycheck can sit against his mortgage, he is assessed DCI at the $190,000 level. As Joey is well aware of this fact, he has been conditioned to allow that $5,000 to sit against his mortgage until he absolutely needs it to begin paying his bills. Keep in mind, given the current $190,000 balance on the mortgage and the lending cap of $220,000, Joey's credit limit immediately increases from $25,000 to $30,000. Better stated, *Joey has a safety net, emergency fund,* or *cushion* of $30,000.

If Joey is astute to his banking system, he will push all of his bills to the latest date possible, so that as much of his $5,000 as possible can sit against his mortgage for as long as possible, saving him DCI.

After letting his $5,000 paycheck sit for a few weeks against his mortgage, it's time for Joey to take $2,000 from his LOC to buy groceries, make his car payments, and pay other bills. This $2000 withdrawal increases his mortgage balance from $190,000 to $192,000 from that day forward, or until he needs more money to pay bills in the ensuing days and weeks. Each time he takes money out, his LOC balance increases.

Over time, Joey has been conditioned to hone his astuteness or awareness of the ever-increasing DCI each time he pulls money out of the LOC. This *conditioning* has changed the way that Joey perceives money and finance. In Joey's mind, whenever he spends money, *it will increase his mortgage balance*; and, he realizes that the day his mortgage balance increases, the DCI assessed that day will also increase. This is the net effect of living out of a debt-account in Australia, as opposed to living out of a cash-account, as we do here in the U.S.

Conversely, in the U.S. our financial conditioning, and therefore perception, is best described as follows: The day we receive our paycheck, we are (metaphorically) wading in dollar bills up to our knees. By the time we pay our mortgage, health insurance, car payments, and credit card bills, the amount of dollar bills has been drawn down to the level of our ankles. But as long as our toes are covered in dollar bills, there are still more dollars to be spent!

The American financial establishment and its institutions have created the perfect consumer thought process: *As long as we have money, we spend it*, and then some, as evidenced by our per capita debt load.

The net result of the Australian system is such that the conditioning comes naturally. It requires little-to-no discipline or sacrifice whatsoever, because the typical mortgage is paid off in 10 years rather than 30. This simple structure cuts $120,000 from Joey's total mortgage-interest bill that would normally be $180,000 in a 30-year mortgage construct.

Let me stress the importance of this $120,000 savings: This is money that remains in Joey's pocket. In projecting this savings over a 10-year period onto a macroeconomic scale, we can realize the following results:

- At Year 10, when the mortgage is paid off: $120,000 begins to spill into the economy, as the consumer is purchasing toys, furniture, cars, rental units, etc., therein bolstering the economy.
- At Year 10, with their mortgage payment removed, the consumer can start funding their retirement much earlier and more aggressively with those freed-up funds.
- Pushing this chunk of mortgage-interest savings back to the consumer creates a substantial boost to the middle class.
- With this level of free-market wealth redistribution and having this money spill into the economy, the Wall Street establishment will have much less influence or impact on the economy, and therefore will experience a substantial decrease in its power to fabricate financial crises.

It is at this point in the workshops that skeptics often say, “the banks will shut it down once they see they are losing this much money.” This has not been the case (to this point) for the simple fact that loans and lines of credit are the bank’s proverbial bread and butter. Within this new financial approach, the homeowner is continually using a LOC.

Moreover, banks know that it is only in a healthy, booming economy, wherein the masses are thriving, that they are most profitable. Conversely, there is little money to be made in a stagnant economy because few can qualify to borrow their money. A person who has their mortgage paid off and has saved $164,000 throughout that mortgage process is more likely to need a larger loan for a new home, for a second home, for a business startup, or for other complex ventures that typically require larger bank loans.

Additionally, given the math behind the mortgage-acceleration concepts, it is now possible to pay off ten mortgages in 30 years, rather than just one. When you can pay a mortgage off in just under 9 years, paying off another mortgage on a second home can occur in just over 7 years for the average client, thanks the added rental income. This period shortens for ensuing home mortgages as massive rental income is generated from mortgage-free properties, rather than creating rental income from properties drowning in mortgage debt.

[Side Bar: For multiple-property owners, there is a wise method for property acquisition, and an extremely unwise method. Leveraging massive mortgage debt to acquire properties, which creates a measly few hundred dollars above the mortgage payment is unwise for many reasons. The most obvious is that too many people lost their multiple-property holdings in 2001 and 2008 because they were far too leveraged, and were one rental vacancy away from negative cash flow.

Advice: Give little credence to the Get-Rich-Quick Real Estate pushers. Real estate acquisition should occur according to some very simple, common sense guidelines far removed from the board game Monopoly.]

Even though the banks are losing two thirds the interest on a mortgage, they are writing many more mortgages over the typical 30-year period, rather than simply one. These mortgages include all the fees for various services from different firms, along with the associated taxes that fund different government agencies, etc. It is for this reason that I coin this approach *a free-market based redistribution of wealth.* However, the banks need to change their paradigms just as much as the consumers in order to expedite this evolution.

THE COMPARISON TO U.S. BANKING

Using the same numbers as our Australian example, let's look at how their system compares to the current mortgage structure in the U.S. in an apples-to-apples comparison. In recapping the numbers, we have a home value of $275,000, which would enable our U.S. consumer—we'll call him Sam—to qualify for a HELOC with a borrowing limit of up to $220,000. With a mortgage balance of $195,000, Sam's credit line is $25,000. And let's say that Sam also has a net income of $5,000/month.

The very day Sam's check is deposited into his checking account, his $5,000 is doing nothing for him as compared to Joey, in Australia. Sam is being dinged with DCI for his mortgage balance of $195,000 until the day that he makes his mortgage payment. By contrast, Joey's mortgage balance was reduced by $5,000 the day his paycheck hit his bank account.

When it comes time to make the mortgage payment, Sam takes $1,000 from his checking account and pays the mortgage.

If Sam's mortgage wasn't due until 3 weeks after his paycheck came in, then his DCI is based on the $195,000 balance for 21 days before his payment reduces his DCI liability. As Sam's payment is $1,000/month; and, in that Sam is in his sixth year of his 30-year mortgage, the ratio of his *interest payment* to his *principle payment* is typically 90/10. The bank takes $900 in the form of interest, with the remaining $100 going toward his principle.

Therefore, the day that Sam makes his mortgage payment, he is credited with $100 of principle—thereby reducing the mortgage from $195,000, down to $194,900. Recapping the interest charges for Sam: For the three weeks that he is waiting to make his $1,000 mortgage payment (21 days), he is assessed DCI on $195,000. For the ensuing 30 days *after* his payment, he is assessed DCI on a $194,900 balance. Joey received a $5,000 credit the day his paycheck came in, and he was assessed DCI on $190,000 until he took money back out of that *open-line mortgage* account to pay his bills. In this typical example, Australians are receiving 50 times more credit in daily calculated interest than their American counterparts.

This is precisely why a 30-year mortgage can be paid off in one third the time, saving two thirds the mortgage interest.

EFFECTIVE MORTGAGE ACCELERATION IN THE U.S.

Using traditional, over-the-counter banking products throughout the past two decades, my clients are achieving better results than the Australian system itself. To illustrate this, I am going to use the same numbers as I used in the previous two models: a net income of $5,000/month, with a $195,000 mortgage.

The first thing we need is a line of credit. It doesn't matter if this is a Personal LOC, a Business LOC, or a *CD-* or *Savings-Secured* LOC (for those with no credit or devastated credit),

[Side Bar: Those trying to establish or re-establish their credit will find that by applying these principles, they can pay off their student loans, car loans, and other consumer debts more quickly, build a financial cushion, and save substantial money in interest.

Additionally, this market sector can build their credit scores and financial reserves much more quickly, putting themselves in a much better position to purchase a home, or finance a business startup more rapidly.]

THE AUSTRALIAN BANKING MODEL IN THE U.S.

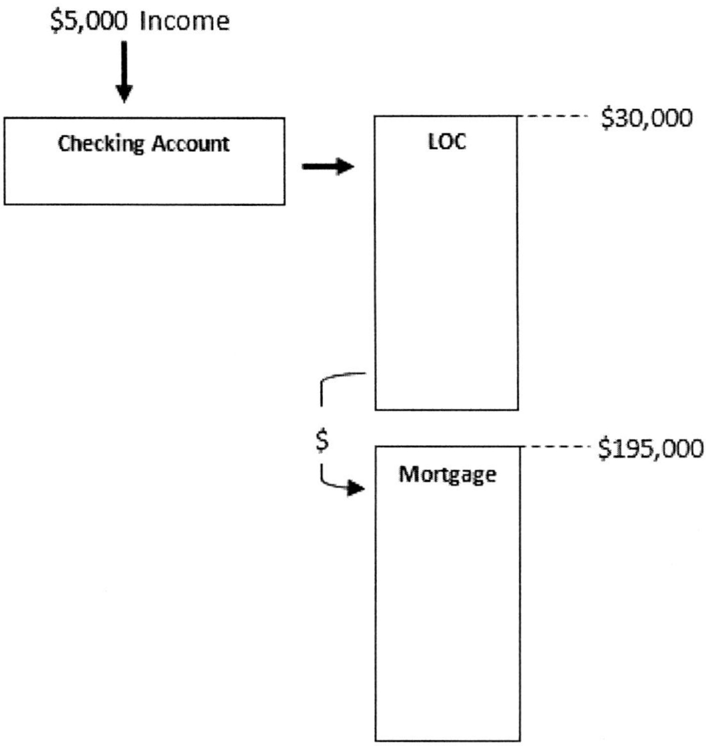

To make this concept work effectively in the U.S., we would first obtain a Home Equity Line of Credit (HELOC) or other LOC. For this example, let's say that we obtained a HELOC with a credit limit of $30,000. In the first transaction, we are going to take a nice, round, easy number of $10,000, withdraw it from the HELOC, and move it against the $195,000 mortgage.

MORTGAGE ACCELERATION: STEP ONE

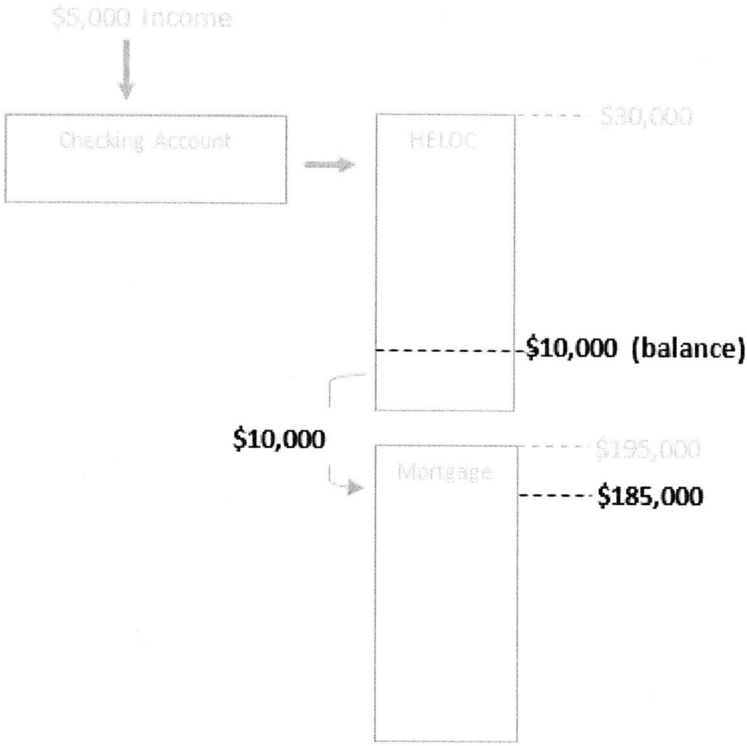

In this first $10,000 transaction, there are some things that I need to point out:

- By taking $10,000 from the HELOC and depositing it against the mortgage, we now have a $10,000 balance in the HELOC for which we are going to start accruing DCI. Always keep in mind that at the stroke of each and every midnight, your DCI is assessed on whatever the balance is; and,

- Because you paid $10,000 against the mortgage, at the stroke of midnight from that day forward, you are paying DCI on a $185,000 balance, rather than on a $195,000 balance.

When teaching CPAs this concept, it is typically at this point that they raise their hand to voice their opposition, with: *When the interest rates for your LOC are higher than the interest rate of your first mortgage, it would be stupid to do this.*

ACCOUNT-RATIO ARBITRAGE

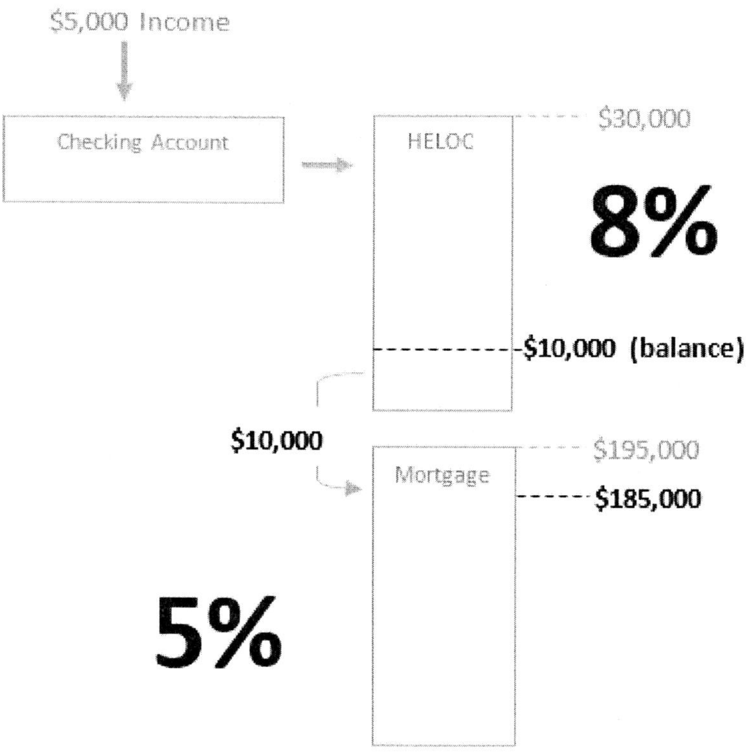

Stated another way:

> *Why would anyone use an 8% LOC to pay down a 5% mortgage?*

This answer is a bit complex, but certainly not rocket science. The most accurate answer to this is: For the most part, interest rates do not matter. Where they *do* matter is on big-ticket items purchased over long periods of time, such as a home mortgage. Moreover, most financial professionals are aware of only four factors of finance:

- **Payment**: The amount of money *and* the intervals in which you are paying back the loan
- **Balance:** The amount of the loan each and every day to which they apply the annual-stated interest rate, which is divided by 365 in order to arrive at DCI
- **Interest Rate:** The rate at which you are paying the bank its interest for lending you the money
- **Time**: The length of the loan

These four factors can, however, be manipulated in various ways. Many consumers have learned to engage in *arbitrage*: the practice of using a more efficient account to pay off a less efficient account. This is often accomplished by using a 0% interest credit card during its introductory period to pay off higher-interest-rate credit cards.

And yet there is another, more effective way to manipulate the four factors of finance. This was discovered early on in the R&D phase, when the interest rates of HELOCs were substantially higher than mortgage interest rates, and yet we were still using the higher-interest-rate HELOCs to pay down the lower-interest-rate mortgages. We call this concept *Account-Ratio Arbitrage* (ARA), which I define as:

> *Using a* ***flexible account*** *with a consistently lower balance that can be manipulated to fluctuate within a consistently lower range than the larger* ***target account;*** *when configured properly, a higher interest rate* ***flexible account*** *can actually and effectively accelerate the pay down of the lower interest-rate* ***target account.***

What CPAs and most mathematically-minded people find most mind boggling is this: the *flexible* HELOC with a higher interest rate can effectively be used to accelerate the *targeted* mortgage or other *targeted* consumer debt—until they *see* the actual math. Most clients have to *experience* this math before they can actually explain it to others. That said, in using the math engine, we can enter an 18% interest rate in the HELOC, and still accelerate a 4% mortgage very effectively, typically pushing the average 8-year and 11-month pay off back another 12 to 16 months.

Citing the previous graph, we took $10,000 from the HELOC, and put that cash against the mortgage. In this first step, we are actually saving 5% on $10,000 (i.e. we are no longer paying 5% on a $195,000 balance, but instead on a $185,000 balance). It is at this point that most CPAs get hung up on paying 8% on the $10,000 balance in the HELOC, yet overlook the fact that there is a $5,000 paycheck that just hit the checking account. Rather than letting that $5,000 paycheck sit in the checking account, with no benefit to the consumer, we move it out of the checking account and into the HELOC, thereby reducing the HELOC balance from $10,000 down to $5,000. Now look at the account ratio: We are saving DCI of 5% on $10,000 in the mortgage, while paying 8% on a $5,000 balance in the HELOC.

MORTGAGE ACCELERATION: STEP TWO

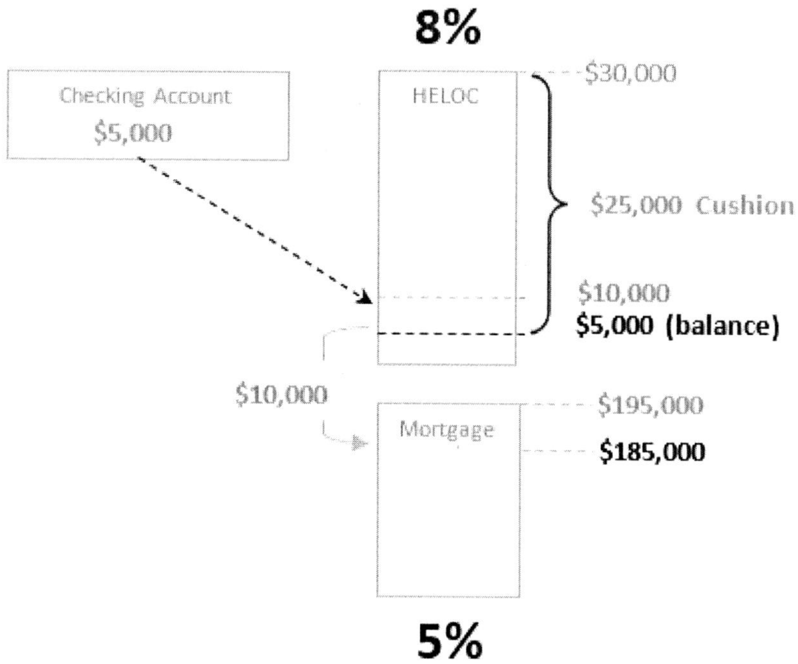

Once again, in the Flexible Account (HELOC) the interest payable is 8% on $5,000, while in the Target Account (Mortgage), the interest savings is 5% on $10,000. This is just the beginning of the ARA concept. At first, the ratio in the HELOC will appear to worsen as the balance grows from $5,000 to $9,000 (or so) as money is withdrawn to pay bills. But keep in mind, this ratio is maintained for only a few days, since your next paycheck is just a few days away.

When the next paycheck comes in, we moved it from the Checking Account into the HELOC. At this point, the $9,000 balance is reduced to $4,000, and the interest-payable ratio is now at 8% on $4,000…all the while, our interest-savings ratio on the mortgage continues to remain steady at a 5% savings on $10,000 throughout this first *cycle*.

Over the course of three to four months, the *principle transfer* amount of $10,000 (for this hypothetical case only), will be paid down to $0, which constitutes the *Bottom of the Cycle*. After reaching the Bottom of the Cycle we repeat the cycle:

MORTGAGE ACCELERATION: STEP TWO

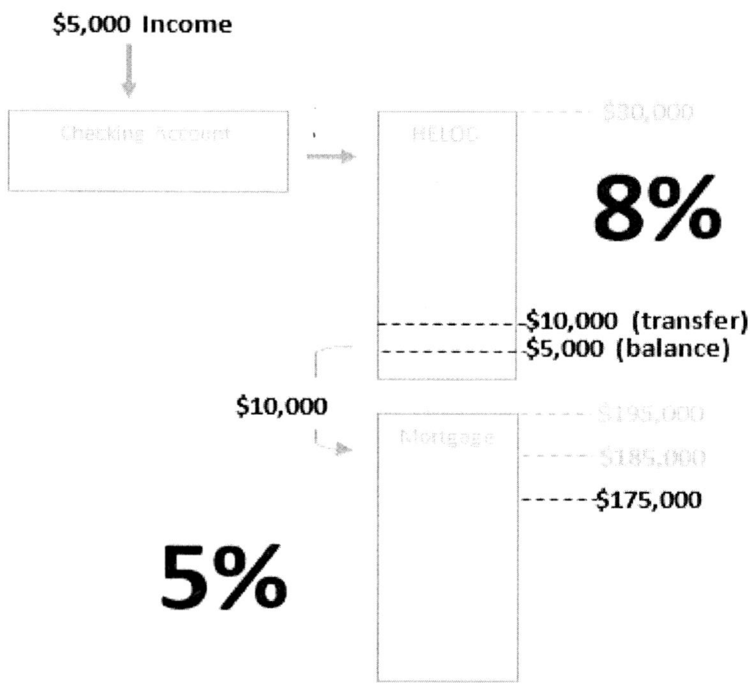

Upon taking the second *principle transfer* of $10,000 and applying it to the mortgage, and after bringing the $5,000 paycheck into the HELOC, the ratios become much more attractive. The flexible account (HELOC) maintains the same interest-payable ratio as it did four months earlier (8% on $5,000); while the target account (mortgage) is now experiencing an interest savings of 5% on $20,000.

The flexible HELOC, which balance fluctuates depending on the manipulation of the principle transfer amount and your paycheck, maintains repetitively low balances as it did through the first cycle. These fluctuating balances will remain consistently low throughout the rest of the cycles. However, the *target* account (mortgage) experiences a massive increase of interest-savings each time another principle transfer is made. This constitutes *Account Ratio Arbitrage*.

As explained previously, it doesn't matter if the HELOC rises to 25%, because by allowing the paycheck to sit against the HELOC balance, we can keep the actual interest payable low for weeks at a time, before having to pay our bills, while exponentially increasing the interest-saving ratio in the *target account*. Therefore, and again, a 25% interest rate in the HELOC, for most consumers, will equate to pushing the average payoff of 8 years and 11 months, back to perhaps 10 years. The account-ratio arbitrage taking place between the two accounts overrides the *perceived* function of the interest rates.

With ARA we are able to bend the long-standing rules of the *Time Value of Money*. This is not to say that the interest rate on the home doesn't matter. If the interest rate on the mortgage were to increase to 25%, this would directly affect the household discretionary income, because the payment becomes much higher. This is why we had such a stagnant economy during the mid-70s when mortgage rates were 18%. And yet even 18% mortgages would not pose a challenge to this approach. Such a high interest rate would however, put homeownership out of the reach of many, just as it did the late 1970s and early 80s.

PAYMENT PERFORMANCE RATIO

The Payment Performance Ratio (PPR) stipulates that the interest rate of a loan is not a determining factor of a good loan.

This discovery arose when a client submitted a financial profile that contained two debts with the same balance of $4,500. One debt was the balance of a car loan, while the second was a credit card balance. The car was a 6% loan, while the credit card was at about 19%. The payment on the car loan was $250/month, while the credit card had a payment of $25/month.

In this actual client math problem, which I will summarize for efficiency, the client had $500/month of discretionary income that we could dedicate to the "additional" payment of these two debts. All we needed to do was determine which debt to apply the $500 discretionary income to first.

Most financial "gurus" would claim that the 19% credit card should be the first to go. However, I'll cut the chase: the most efficient and safe pay down of these two debts would be to apply the $500/month against the 6% car first.

By applying the $500/month discretionary income to the $250 car payment first, the car is paid off in just over six months, <u>at which point</u>

he now has $750/month discretionary income, after freeing up the $250/month car payment. Compare this to paying the 19% credit card first: If you were to reverse the order and pay off the 19% credit card first, it will require 9 months to pay it off, $500/month plus the $25/month credit card payment. At the end of the nine-month period, you have only increased your discretionary income from $500/month to $525/month by freeing up the credit card payment.

- **Lower-Interest Car First:** By paying off the 6% car loan first in 6 months, you then have $750 in monthly discretionary income to add to the current $25/month credit card payment; you can pay the credit card off in another 6 months (12 months for paying off both debts).
- **Higher-Interest Credit Card First:** By paying off the 19% credit card loan first in 9 months, you then have $525 in monthly discretionary income to add to the current $250/month car payment. You can pay the $3117 remaining car balance off in another 6 months (15 months for paying off both debts).

As a general rule, you want to free up the most cash as soon as possible. In this case, we can increase the discretionary cash from $500/month to $750 at month six by paying off the car first, rather than opting for the smaller increase of discretionary income from $500/month to $525 at month nine by paying the higher-interest credit card bill off first.

In some instances where the two interest rates are closer together, you will be weighing the value of spending a few more dollars in interest in order to free up more cash sooner.

From this concept, I was then able to extrapolate a general rule of thumb which better determined *good* and *bad* debts, and better yet, devised the means by which debts could be prioritized or ranked so that the worst (or least efficient) debts could be paid off first. I call this formulation the *Payment Performance Ratio* (PPR).

Based on the premise that *increased cash flow almost always takes precedence over APR* (interest rate), we take the ratio between the balance and the payment to determine which creditor is giving us the *most dollars for the least payment*: In the example of the car and the credit card, the car created an 18-to-1 ratio, while the credit card was a 180-to-1 ratio. This meant that for *every dollar I paid to the car company each month, the car financier was lending me $18*. Whereas, every *dollar I paid to the credit card company each month, they were lending me $180*. Generally, the higher the ratio, the better the loan.

Because of current mortgage and HELOC rates, these constitute some of the most efficient debt vehicles, with PPRs ranging from 100-to-1 to 300-to-1.

Conversely, people will boast about how they got a 0% interest loan on their car over a 6-year period, however the payment is somewhere in the $600 to $900/month range (most often, more of a car payment than they can afford). When you divide the debt by the monthly payment of these 0%-interest transactions, the PPRs are somewhere below the 50-to-1 ratio—typically a "bad" or "low-efficiency" or "very expensive" debt—regardless the interest rate. So often, this puts the consumer in a very tight or precarious position that is most often justified with, "But I am paying 0% interest!" In most cases, especially during the deep recessions, many people in this "precarious position" would have been better off paying a bit of interest and having smaller payments, rather having their car repossessed because they couldn't afford the larger interest-free payments.

So once again, with the mortgage- or debt-acceleration approach, *cash is king*; or, having as much of your paycheck as possible sitting against your debt for as long as possible. This is what makes the concept work. If you are paying $900/month for a car because you were enticed by the 0%-interest ploy, when your paycheck actually dictates you should not be spending more than $600/month for a car payment, you have $300 less *per month* sitting against your *strategic* debt (the HELOC in this case), and you are often preempted from engaging in debt acceleration altogether.

> [Side Bar: The examples as exhibited throughout this chapter are based on simplified math for easy illustration purposes.
>
> Please note, regarding the $10,000 *principle transfer* amount: the *principle transfer amount* <u>is not a one-size-fits-all figure</u>. The configuration is a combination of specific amounts paid on scheduled intervals that are unique to each individual. As an individual's income and expenses will change with the ebbs and flows of life, so too will their pay off schedule.]

FOR THE SKEPTICS

Skeptics will often quip: Why not just put your money into a savings account (therein generating interest), and when the balance arrives close to the correct "principle transfer amount," then simply put that money against the mortgage? In this manner, you are "making interest" in the savings account, rather than paying interest in the HELOC. This argument is flawed on many levels:

- If such an idea worked, then why don't banks operate this way? They work from credit and credit lines. If you want to become like the bank, then act and operate like a bank: rather than doing what Ma 'n Pa told you to do.
- It requires much more discipline to save money <u>and not spend it</u>. Case in point: 200 years of history of American spending/saving habits. If it worked effectively, then the majority of consumers would be doing it. Why aren't they? So historically, saving money and placing it against debt has not worked.
- Placing a large chunk of money against a 5% mortgage saves you 5% interest on that chunk of money immediately. Your paycheck then sits against the debt (in the HELOC) reducing interest payable on the amount that you withdrew, in order to place it against the mortgage. Conversely, by placing money in a savings account and waiting for that money to grow, you are only earning 1% or less as it accumulates AND paying

interest on the entire mortgage balance, rather than on the reduced mortgage balance.

- Placing money against the mortgage without some means of getting it back (should you need it) is risky because of foreclosure. The HELOC serves as a *buffer,* which allows you to access the money should a financial hardship occur.
- By using the savings account, you are allowing the bank to take 94% of your funds from both your checking account and the savings account, when in fact all that money—all year long, could be sitting against *your* mortgage, thereby saving you much more interest than you are spending, because of *Account Ratio Arbitrage.*
- Therefore, instead of surrendering this cash to the bank, and more precisely *to the banker*, where it will be placed against the bank's debt accounts, consumers can preempt this action by placing it against *their* debts.

The savings-account postulation simply cannot compete, nor has it since the inception of banking. *Having cash on hand* for emergencies is a different story: a sermon for another day.

THE MORTGAGE-INTEREST DEDUCTION MYTH

A less-than-credible objection to this approach to finance, often maintained by CPAs, is:

If I or my clients pay off their mortgages, then they will lose their Mortgage-Interest Deduction, the biggest write-off that the IRS allows.

Before getting into the simple math behind this misperception, let me first state a general rule of thumb when it comes to taxes is:

The only thing better than a tax write-off is not having to pay the bill at all.

The mortgage-interest deduction is *not* a dollar-for-dollar reduction of your overall *tax liability*. Rather, it is a reduction of your gross income, which reduces the taxes.

In the tax-preparation process, the average citizen takes his *gross income*, then subtracts the various write-offs allowed by the IRS from the gross income, arriving at the amount of *taxable income*. The first table shows the taxes a homeowner would pay with a mortgage (wherein this homeowner is paying $10K/year in mortgage interest to the bank), while the second table is indicative of a homeowner whose mortgage is paid off.

Taxes with a Mortgage (Paying $10K in Interest to the Bank)

1	Gross Income	$60,000.00
2	Mortgage-Interest Write-Off	$10,000.00
3	Taxable Income	$50,000.00
4	**Tax Liability (at 20%)**	**$10,000.00**

Taxes without a Mortgage (Paying $0 to the Bank)

1	Gross Income	$60,000.00

2	Mortgage-Interest Write-Off	$0
3	Taxable Income	$60,000.00
4	**Tax Liability (at 20%)**	**$12,000.00**

The homeowner *with a mortgage*, pays $10,000 in taxes, while the homeowner *without a mortgage* pays $12,000. However, the homeowner *without* a mortgage paid $0 to the bank in the form of interest, while the mortgaged homeowner paid $10,000 to the bank in order to receive his $2,000 "savings". After taxes, the homeowner whose mortgage is paid off is $8,000 ahead of his mortgaged counterpart.

It simply makes no sense to pay a bank $10,000 in interest so that you receive a $2,000 reduction in taxes. Once again, this is a net loss of $8,000. It makes much more sense to pay off your mortgage, pay the extra $2,000 in taxes, and pocket the remaining $8,000 that was previously flowing to the bank. We have been conditioned to embrace this mortgage-interest deduction myth due to conditioning by generations of professionals.

Under our current financial system and given our current tax code: A *tax deduction* is not a reason to *remain* in debt. Pay off your debts and pay the relatively small difference in taxes.

FORECLOSURE PROTECTION

Besides paying off your mortgage earlier and saving an average of $164,000 in mortgage interest, there are so many other benefits to this structure. A secondary benefit is the protection it provides against foreclosure. As you can see, we have now completed our first three cycles, paying $30,000 toward our $195,000 sample mortgage, over a nine to twelve-month period. Eventually, you may want to go back to the bank and expand the original $30,000 HELOC to include the additional $30,000 of *new* home equity—increasing the HELOC limit to $60,000.

HELOC PRE-EXPANSION

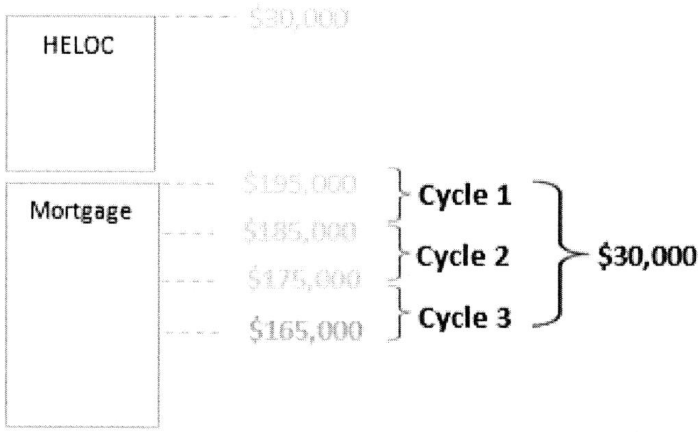

HELOC POST-EXPANSION

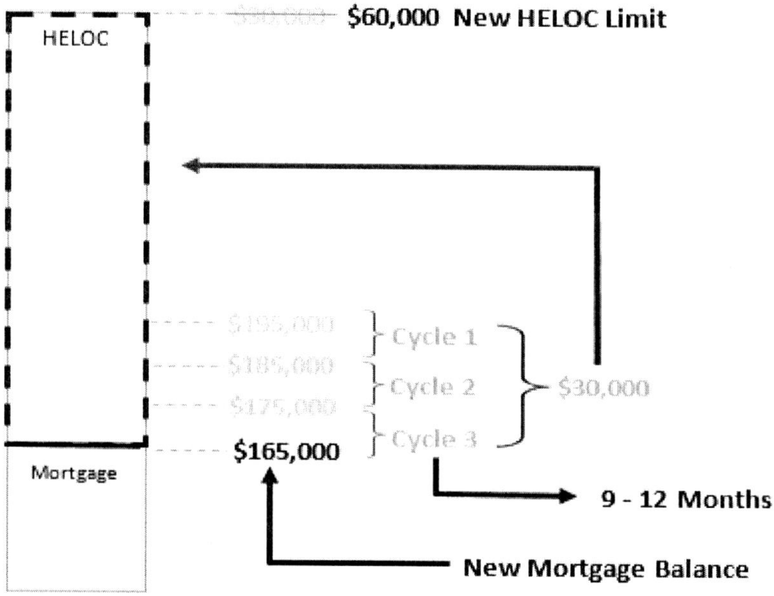

This expanding "cushion" of the HELOC becomes a safety net—a safety net that actually saved many of my clients during the 2008 recession from losing their homes. If you were injured or laid off from work and facing foreclosure, typically you have 90 days of missed mortgage payments before the banks begin foreclosing on your home (i.e. have you evicted and sell the home). However, by continuing to expand the HELOC, you have an extensive "cushion" with which to pay your mortgage and living expenses while getting back on your feet.

Along these lines, I highly recommend that individuals avoid 15-year mortgages, unless they have plenty of reserves to get them through a downturned economy or personal tragedy. With a 15-year mortgage, you are legally on the hook for a much larger payment. With this new mortgage-acceleration approach, it is much more safe and sensible to obtain a 30-year, or even a 40-year, mortgage, so that you are contractually responsible for a much smaller payment.

In this manner, you then have the option to accelerate the payments as both safety and common sense dictates, protected against the possibility of foreclosure.

CHAPTER 3

The Failed Retirement Structures

TO FULLY APPRECIATE THE VALIDITY and viability of your retirement fund, and of your overall retirement strategy, let's start with an assessment of the two retirement systems in the U.S., which are:

- Pensions
- Pre-tax or tax-deferred accounts (e.g. 401(k)s, IRAs, 403(b)s, etc.)

The *pension* structure became popular in the 1950s and began to decline and fail in the mid-1980s, specifically when *managerial capitalism* was replaced with *finance capitalism.*

[Side Bar: Under managerial capitalism, there was more of a partnership between the company and its employees. In this implied partnership, employees would dedicate their careers and lives to a company, after which the company would provide that employee both a wage throughout their career, as well as a retirement, via a pension.

Under finance capitalism, the CEO and company board evolved into fiduciaries for the shareholders, rather than for the employees. Their primary objective became shareholder profits.]

Despite the evolution of capitalism however, both the private sector and the judiciary saw, early on, the pension structure was not sustainable for these companies. By the early 1990s, most companies had replaced the pension structure with the Pre-Tax, or Tax-Deferred Structure.

As per the failure of the Pre-Tax Structure, through the past 10 years the leading authorities who developed and championed this structure are now condemning it as a failure, as do the government agencies and tens of thousands of online and traditional news-reporting agencies. But you don't have to take their word for it. You need only look at your 401(k) or IRA, and measure its consistent rise and fall through the past two decades. Let's assess these one at a time.

Starting with pensions, there are three basic pension sectors:

- The Private Sector, comprised of private corporations and businesses
- The Public Sector, comprised of governments or government agencies and departments
- Social Security, which is a nationalized pension

PRIVATE SECTOR PENSIONS

In the 1980s, the private sector came to realize the unsustainable nature of pensions. As a result, companies began filing Chapter 11, a specific type of bankruptcy wherein all players attempt to keep the business alive by restructuring or completely dismissing company debt.

> [Side Bar: In fairness to the jilted pensioners, many of these companies may have engaged in poor business practices that resulted in losses, thereby putting the company in a position where it could no longer fund its pension program. Or, just like government does from time to time, some companies may have raided their pension funds, or simply stopped the flow of revenue into the allocated accounts, thereby hastening their demise.]

Regardless of the cause, the crux of the solution for the private sector boiled down to one choice for the judiciary: Do we dissolve the company and sell off its assets in order to pay the pensions of former employees? Or, do we dismiss the pension debts and allow the company to stay in business, which helps keep the economy going, and keeps individuals working and making a living? History shows that the judiciary has typically ruled in favor of the *newlyweds* over the *nearly-deads*—a cold, harsh reality.

As a result, the private sector began replacing pensions with the Pre-Tax/Tax-Deferred Structure—the 401(k) becoming its crown jewel. The rationale for changing to this structure was: If the market lost, the retirement accounts lost. The company was no longer responsible for providing past employees with guaranteed retirement payments, or being the guarantors of guaranteed retirements.

Keep in mind that a company would have to make payments for their retired employees regardless of the financial state of that company or of the economy. This unsustainability is obvious: The company must be unceasingly profitable to viably fund a sustainable pension. For companies to be profitable, the economy must be stable and growing. Ergo, pension programs are dependent on a good economy and a profitable company. Do companies struggle and/or fail? Yes. Does the economy affect the performance of companies? Yes. Does the economy ever experience downturns that last for three to four years? Yes. Lastly, if companies are required to make guaranteed pension payments, then who is going to guarantee the economy against recession or depression? Or, who is going to guarantee company profits for that matter, so that it can, in turn, guarantee payments to its pensioners?

And yet a few large companies felt they could weather any economic storm, and continued offering pensions of their own volition, many of which have since failed. As an additional safeguard against lost pensions, the government set up the Pension Benefits Guarantee Corporation (PBGC), which collected premiums from these companies. This corporation and fund serves as a backup should any PBGC-backed company fail.

As of August 2010, U.S. News and World Report ran a story entitled, *The 10 Biggest Failed Pension Plans*; these were *private-sector* pensions. The first line reads: *Pension plans abandoned by just ten companies make up 63% of all claims paid out by the Pension Benefits*

Guarantee Corp. The article then lists the companies and the billions of dollars they cannot pay to pensioners. Keep in mind, these are private-sector companies that continued down this unsustainable path for an additional 25 years after most of the private sector discovered the flaw, and made the switch.

This concept alone speaks volumes about the knowledge base (or lack thereof) of the Chief Financial Officers (CFOs) as well as the CEOs, Board Members, and other financial "gurus" of these companies. A sustainable "guaranteed" pension is only as good as the economy.

For consumers on pensions who put forth both thought and effort into planning for their retirement, a popular trend to keep in mind and plan for is cited on the PBGC's own website:

> *The maximum pension benefit guaranteed by PBGC is set by law and adjusted yearly. For plans that end in 2016, the maximum guarantee for workers who retire at age 65 is $60,136 yearly ($5,011.36 monthly).*

Pensions can and do reduce pension disbursement in order to keep the pension alive.

As mentioned in the *U.S. News* article, auto-technology provider *Delphi* was one of those ten companies that continued its pension program. Upon its failure in 2009, the PBGC was responsible for $6.1 billion in benefits to its approximate 69,000 workers and retirees, or about $88,000/year per retiree. As per the PBGC policy (above), which sets a maximum payment of *$60,136/year*, it appears that PBGC's "yearly adjustments" to the Delphi pensions constitutes a 25%

reduction—far less than what these pensioners were planning for. And yet with another 24,000 pension plans shared by 40 million Americans backed by the PBGC, *reduced retirements* will be the trend until this "guarantee fund" itself is no longer sustainable—no different than Social Security.

The increased number and pace of pension failures will determine if, indeed, there will be any payment or benefit at all. Learning from history, in the 1980s when companies filed for bankruptcy, there were typically $0 payouts to pensioners. When you add the inevitable collapse of the enormous public pension structures to these relatively small private-pension failures, not only will the payments stop, but this "Pension Bubble" will rival the "2008 Mortgage Bubble" in magnitude and devastation.

> [Side Bar: I have personally met with and talked to individuals who have enjoyed their retirements for the past 20 years, unable to "connect" with this message of "pension doom." There *are* relatively few pensions that have kept their proverbial heads above the waterline. However, these are typically found in specialty sectors such as institutions of higher education. The reason these pensions have done well is because of the robust profit margins of these institutions. (Remember, it requires both *company profitability* as well as a healthy *economy* to properly and *consistently* fund a pension plan). In reference to higher education specifically, you've had a steady customer pool of 16,000 to 30,000 students per

university who have easily-accessible, low-interest government money, which flows freely and quickly to these schools. Additionally, because of government funding, schools are a recession-proof industry. Of course, these pensions are going to be healthily funded! But their days are numbered as is their income source (the Federal Student Loan structure), as we are also nearing a "Student Loan Bubble" with large loan defaults and Student-Loan Forgiveness programs.

Moreover, the students/customers themselves have wised up to taking out $100,000 in loans for a degree in Fine Arts, only to end up flipping hamburgers for the ensuing 5 to 10 years, often defaulting on these loans. This corrective curve will eventually catch up to these unsustainable pensions too.]

PUBLIC PENSIONS AND THE LOOMING FALLOUT

It is extremely important to understand that failing pensions directly affect everyone, whether you have a pension or not. As a tax-paying United States citizen, you will eventually end up footing the bill for their failure. In most states where pensions are failing, they are recouping those losses by extracting them from the homeowner, by way of *non-asset bonds* tacked on to property taxes.

As either a taxpayer or a voter, this material is relevant and financially crucial, especially when you come to realize that you are, most likely, on the hook for the underfunded retirements of *future* public workers, as well as unfunded retirements of *past* city workers. The underfunded nature has many causes: 1) the flawed structure itself, based on flawed math 2) civic mismanagement, bad policy, gaping loopholes for cheaters who misuse the system, etc.; and 3) fraud, embezzlement, lack of management skills and other inefficiencies of the administrators.

If the unfunded pension obligations are being paid for in the form of non-asset bonds, then the taxpayer base is also paying interest to finance these retirement tabs of others. This is extremely crucial to you because the amount due by each taxpayer is reaching the point that it is hindering those trying to purchase a home. It endangers those struggling to pay for their homes, especially those on fixed incomes. Finally, it hinders others from funding their own retirements because they are paying for the retirements of someone else—stealthily loaded on the backs of homeowners—i.e. THE MIDDLE CLASS!

> [Side Bar: Let's address these non-asset bonds in a bit more detail.
>
> Let's say that a state's pension administrator was receiving funds from its cities for the pensions of all the city workers, police, firemen, teachers, etc. Through mismanagement and lack of ability to negotiate properly with these municipal workers' unions, the cities begin missing payments to the pension administrator.
>
> Before long, the city's past-due payments reach $20 million because these pension payments were spent on other things, rather than being sent to the pension administrator.

To remedy the mismanagement by the city government, they apply for a bond, which means they borrow the $20 million from the bank, wherein interest is assessed. Once this debt is on the city's books, they must now allocate a portion of their limited revenue, derived from taxes, which means the city has raise taxes or cut other services. Typically, they simply charge each household its "share" of the bond by creating a new line-item tax entry on your tax bill.

If you cannot pay the tax, then the city levies a tax lien on your home. If you don't pay that, then they can foreclose on your home (i.e. forcing you to sell your home in order to extract the taxes due).]

In California, depending on which set of books you have access to, the per-household share of these retirement debts is nearing the $60,000. As reported in the New York Times, pensions typically have two sets of books: one for themselves, and the other for the government and public, as documented in *A Sour Surprise for Public Pensions: Two Sets of Books* (New York Times, Walsh, Sept 17, 2016).

[Side Bar: My portion of these failing pensions on a property in the state of California is currently $1,000/**year**—assessed on my property taxes *exclusively* for the past unfunded portions of the retirement debts. This is in addition to the approximate $1,000/**month** for the actual property taxes, about 90% of which pays for the current city employees' wages, *current* retirement payments for *current* workers, and other services. Unfortunately, our politicians are continually proposing more bonds to fund these "guaranteed" retirement payments for public workers—most often resulting from their mismanagement. And as these municipal employers are falling further behind in their pension-obligation payments, the elected officials simply push for more bonds while consistently raising pensions rather than negotiating into something more sustainable; while providing the best medical benefits—most often exceeding those in the private sector.

So again, this is a crucial taxpayer and voter issue, unless you have no problem contributing to someone else's retirement account rather than your own—all because of a faulty structure that no one will step up and correct…until now.]

Interestingly, many states and municipalities also saw the unsustainable nature of pensions, and when the private sector began abandoning them, many states and municipalities followed suit, transitioning their employee pensions into 401(k)s or other pre-tax/tax-deferred accounts.

Unfortunately, many of these states and municipalities zagged, and maintained the overwhelming burden of the pension structure, putting their citizens on the hook to pay the shortfall of these "guaranteed" pensions.

Expounding on the ramifications of the public-pension debacle, let's return to my $1,000/year Pension Bond previously cited. The tax-extracting techniques to make up for fund-mismanagement is not unique to me or my fellow residents. Nearly half of the states are facing pension shortfalls.

In California, most municipalities belong to the California Public Employees Retirement System (CalPERS). Those participating cities pay their employees a wage, offer a health plan, and they contribute a specified amount of money to CalPERS for each employee (along with the employees' contributions). The role of CalPERS, as a fiduciary to the pensioners, is to take the money and increase it through investment for the benefit of each employee, much like a 401(k) administrator. However, rather than strictly adhering to the traditional fiduciary role, CalPERS has engaged in trendy *green-* or *responsible*-investing strategies. These strategies have often resulted in too many losses, which are exacerbated by frequent economic corrections.

> [Side Bar: Referencing *finance capitalism*, where the CEO and a company board have a fiduciary responsibility to the shareholders or, where investment brokers have a fiduciary responsibility to their clients: Government agencies are not under the same duty, or pressure to perform, as is the private sector. As a norm, government workers, or the fund administrators in this case, cannot be fired. They are paid the same wage regardless of their performance, their absence, or the performance of the fund itself. In the case of lost funds due

to ineptness, fraud, embezzlement, or market correction, the responsibility to pay the shortfall remains solely on the backs of the home- or property-owning taxpayers.]

Additionally, with a lack of oversight, CalPERS principals have engaged in embezzlement and fraud for personal gain and gluttony, losing millions of dollars—at least that we know of. Add to this the mismanagement of municipalities that fall short in their payments to CalPERS, creating an ever-increasing and overwhelming debt load on our already-struggling middle class.

In 2009, I was presenting to a group in downtown Oakland, CA, which included a few teachers. They claimed that their pension fund was doing great. Yet having just experienced the 2008 crash, this didn't seem feasible or possible, and I openly stated as much. Two years later, the California State Comptroller released a report stating that CalPERS, along with the California State Teacher's Retirement System (CalSTRS), were underfunded by $101 billion.

This report also stated that at this same time, California's entire operating budget was $89 billion annually (i.e. the amount to keep the state running via wages for firefighting, flood/disaster control, road construction, maintenance, and repair; all the social and medical services, etc.). In other words, the amount needed to simply bring the retirement fund back to a healthy breakeven point, would require $12 billion up and above the operating budget for the entire state.

Since then, this $101 billion shortage has grown anywhere from $400 billion to $900 billion depending on the reporting source, the reporting agency's political outlook, which set of books you have access to, and/or their accounting methodologies.

With another economic downturn as the result of, say, a Pension Bubble, these pension-fund deficits will increase again. Therefore, investment strategies alone will never erase these deficits. Their viability is directly tied to the economy. When the economy fails, the taxpayers must, once again, pay the bill for the few, elite, guaranteed retirements, rather than into their own. When assessing what this translates into dollar-wise, keep in mind what this means for *you* specifically in *your* state.

At the $500 billion underfunded mark, each person (man, woman, and child) in the state of California would be responsible for $12,820 of the current retirement fund liabilities of these two pensions. If and/or when the liability reaches $900 billion, which some project it to be already, the per-capita responsibility would increase to $23,076.

However, because the mechanism for enforcing payment for this public-worker retirement liability is property taxes, we then need to transition from a per capita share into a household share. In that there are approximately 14 million households in California, and given a liability of $500 billion, the per-household liability grows to $35,714, while a $900 billion deficit equates to a $64,285 per-household.

To truly appreciate the unsustainable nature of this problem, one simply needs to consider how long it will take the average homeowner to pay off an additional $30,000 to $60,000 of debt, while to trying to pay off his/her mortgage AND fund his/her own retirement. With unions, inept politicians, and government ideologues continuing to insist that ordinary citizens pay for the mismanagement of these pensions, citizens are unable to contribute to their own retirements. These tax payments currently rival many mortgage payments. And with each economic correction, embezzlement episode, and/or ill-negotiated contract, the proverbial can is simply kicked down the road as we continually increase these per-household share of the retirement burden of others.

[Side Bar: The $35,000 to $65,000 per-household deficit becomes even more pronounced when you consider that approximately 55% of households in California are owner-occupied housing. The other 45% is made up of renter-occupied apartments. This would mean that landlords would have to raise the rent exponentially "if everyone is to pay their fair share of these retirement plans."

This poses a big problem for many cities with rent control measures. With such ordinances on the books, landlords would not be able to increase the rents, and therefore, *they* would be responsible for a larger share, easily putting this industry out of business.

In turn, this would put the squeeze back on to the single-family homeowners via the property-tax collection mechanism to collect the amount that just morphed into $70,000 on the low side, and $120,000 on the high—because renters either cannot afford it, or are protected by rent-control measures. Once again, the net effect is a huge financial burden placed squarely on the back of the middle- class homeowners.]

Before moving on to the next section, it is worth noting that this battle of "guaranteed pensions for public workers at the expense of others" is now playing out in the bankruptcy courts, wherein the courts are deferring the decision back to the voters.

In the recent bankruptcy proceedings for the California municipalities of San Bernardino and Stockton, the federal bankruptcy court granted these cities the option to have the pension liabilities dismissed. The State of California argued that state law did not allow cities to dismiss its pension obligations to CalPERS or CalSTRS. The court returned with, *state laws do not override federal bankruptcy laws*. Therefore, the decision whether to dismiss the pension obligations was left up to the voters by referendum.

If the citizens choose to dismiss the obligations, they can once again concentrate on funding their own retirements rather than funding the retirements of their public workers. If these voters decide to maintain and honor these pension debts, this ugly cycle will continue to the point where tax-lien foreclosures will either create Detroit-type ghost towns, or bring about hypergentrification. By upholding this failed system, the political left and unions (such as SEIU), who claim to abhor gentrification and the displacement of the poor and middle class, are creating their own monster.

States and municipalities that have phased out employee pensions, and transitioned their employees over to the retirement vehicles of the private sector (401Ks, IRAs, etc.) are not only better off financially than those which kept the pension structure, but also these municipalities are not putting these massive and unsustainable burdens on their taxpayer base mostly comprised of the middle class.

If you have a pension, I would recommend diversifying your retirement strategy for the fact that it is simply unsustainable. If you are not able to fund your retirement because you are currently funding the pensions of others through your property taxes, I would suggest you join citizen-based tax associations and movements to fight this disturbing trend, and politically or legally force a fair resolution to this elitist travesty. Bottom line: It is the least efficient wealth-redistribution model on the planet [i.e. hundreds of billions of redistributed dollars (in the case of CALPERS) paying for the retirements of less than 1.5 million workers].

SOCIAL SECURITY

In 1935, the Federal government expanded the pension concept further by creating the Social Security program. Upon its inception, there were approximately 45 workers paying into the system per one (1) beneficiary pulling retirement from the system. Today, that 45-to-1 ratio has fallen to 2.3 workers for every beneficiary on the program. Adding this to the endless report from all agencies predicting when the Social Security funds will be depleted, we don't need to belabor its imminent failure.

Interestingly and pertaining to its demise, there have been two notable and plausible proposed fixes to the program: *Means Testing* and *Nationalized (Socialized) Retirement.*

Means Testing is a measurement process by which analysts assess *who* could feasibly receive *how much* from the system, premised on how much money an individual or couple was making (or is being disbursed from their "other, non-Social Security" retirement accounts) in order to determine how long the fund could remain viable before lapsing or collapsing. Hillary Clinton said it best during her 2008 campaign with the adage, "If you don't need it, you lose it."

Originally, lawmakers tested the $100,000 level, meaning, if a household (husband and wife, either separately or together) made $100,000, then they would not receive any Social Security payments. However, when the lawmakers ran the numbers they discovered that not enough people were making $100,000. Therefore, that "$100,000 disqualification mark" did little to prolong the life of the program.

The lawmakers then reduced the earning cap from $100,000 to the $50,000 level. In other words, despite paying into the program your entire working life, if as a household, you were drawing more than $50,000/year from your retirement fund, on which to live, you would not receive your Social Security benefits.

The proponents of *Means Testing* have, for the most part, gone silent. There are now mumblings echoing from the D.C. lawmaking chambers about nationalized retirement.

Because of the unending scandals, rampant fraud, and the trillions in lost retirement dollars by Wall Street, lawmakers have their eye on the $23 trillion in the private retirement accounts of American workers.

It is not only very possible, but quite feasible for the federal government to confiscate this $23 trillion, pay off the $20 trillion national debt (resetting its proverbial credit card balance back to $0), save Social Security, and bail out the failing public pensions in one fell swoop.

Some have countered with, "You will have 65 million screaming-mad Americans who won't let it happen" (i.e. those with a 401(k), IRA, or other robust private retirement accounts). However, keep in mind that we are a democracy. There are another 150 million voting Americans who don't have a substantial amount in their retirement accounts, who *would* benefit from this plausible government grab. Such a campaign would come down to one very crucial question: *Who do you trust more with your retirement money, Wall Street or the government?* I would surmise that the majority of Americans would vote government over Wall Street. It's a tossup!

Moreover, government has a substantial claim on these private retirement funds (at least 20% or more) as these funds have not yet been taxed. Remember, they are all tax-deferred funds. The government would be somewhat "justified" in grabbing, at minimum, a quarter of this fund (e.g. $5 trillion) in the face of a financial collapse. They have been doing this with the G-Fund for decades. The G-Fund is the retirement fund for federal workers, which the federal government has been dipping into to cover shortfalls during cash crunches.

Regardless of the side of this issue on which you find yourself, it would behoove you to become educated on this and all other financial issues surrounding retirement, and then act accordingly. It could very well determine your life and lifestyle throughout your retirement years.

If you are not putting, or have not put away sufficient money for your retirement, and you think that nationalized retirement is a windfall that will provide you with enough money on which to live, then think again. With everyone going on the program, including those in failing public pensions, the per capita share (i.e. your nationalized pension) will be miniscule—a very unfortunate chain of events for the metaphoric ants who worked day and night while the grasshoppers fiddled.

THE PRE-TAX / TAX-DEFERRED STRUCTURE

The Pre-Tax Structure has also failed miserably. This *absolute failure* is no longer vague, abstract writing on the wall. It has been documented and printed by nearly every reputable news agency in the nation, denounced by its original proponents, and reported by the Federal Treasury.

The Federal Treasury Report of 2012 states that the average household net worth from 1992 to 2010 was stagnant at $77,000. This figure was derived from home equity and retirement accounts (namely, 401(k)s and IRAs), painting a bleak picture of zero-growth in both of these sectors. When transposing the net results of this report onto actual 401(k)-performance models, they also show zero growth for this same period of time.

More specifically, the 1992 net-worth figure of $77,000 rose to $126,000 over the course of 15 years (2007). Not an impressive feat whatsoever, as money on the S&P 500 typically doubles every 9 or so years. In this case, the money only increased 63% over this 15-year period, just over 4% annually (before taxes and admin fees). What is more devastating however, is the fact that three years later, the measly 4% annual increase was completely wiped out, returning once again to the $77,000 level—the same level as 1992. Americans lost 18 years (i.e. over a third) of their typical 45-year retirement-investment window.

> [Side Bar: These 18 years of lost time (1992-2010) are expanded for the Age 55-64 demographic when we expand the data set from 1989 to 2013. As reported in the Wall Street Journal (Feb. 16, 2017), the average net worth of this demographic has fallen from $175,300 in 1989 to $168,900 in 2013. This constitutes 24 years—nearly a quarter-century—of lost time in these fruitless retirement vehicles, as per The Federal Reserve Survey of Consumer Finances: Center of Economic and Policy Research.]

Though this is big news, it is nothing *new.* We came to this conclusion in the 2001 recession and again in 2008. Any gains in these accounts were eventually wiped out—and everyone and their dog have been reporting on this failure. Case in point: If you were to type the words "401k failure" into a search engine, it results in 400,000 to

500,000 articles. The following constitutes a small sampling of those top results:

- ***For Millions of Americans, the 401(k) is a failure,*** *CNBC.com*, Mar. 23, 2015
- ***Why 401(k)s Have Failed,*** *Forbes*, Apr. 24, 2013
- ***401(k) Plans Are Failing Retirees,*** *Newsmax*, June 27, 2012
- ***A Perfect Failure: Why the 401(k) Has Been a Flop,*** *Huffington Post*, June 7, 2012
- ***Here's Why Your 401(k) Is a Failure,*** *Los Angeles Times*, Nov. 9, 2010
- ***Why the 401(k) Is a Failed Experiment,*** *PBS*, Apr. 23, 2013
- ***The Retirement Revolution That Failed: Why the 401(k) Isn't Working***, *Yahoo Finance*, Mar. 4, 2016

The two most authoritative assessments of the 401(k) to hit the newsstands consist are made by the original promoters and backers of the 401(k) who now publicly admit to the failure, misrepresentation, and the unintended results of the failed pre-tax concept. These articles are:

- ***The Inventor of the 401(k) Says He Created a Monster,*** *MarketWatch*, Sept. 2016

- ***The Champions of the 401(k) Lament the Revolution They Started****,* *Wall Street Journal*, Jan. 3, 2017, by Timothy Martin.

This most recent Wall Street Journal article of January 3, 2017 encapsulates everything I have been teaching throughout the past two decades regarding the fallacy of the Pre-Tax Structure. Let's assess the new capitulations of the former proponents of the 401(k). It will serve as a good foundation for the ensuing chapters.

> *Many early backers of the 401(k) now say they have regrets about how their creation turned out despite its emergence as the dominant way most Americans save. Some say it wasn't designed to be a primary retirement tool and acknowledge they used forecasts that were too optimistic to sell the plan...*

Thus far, we see that the 401(k), "wasn't designed to be a primary retirement tool", and yet for some reason, it has evolved for the most part, into the *de facto retirement tool.*

A larger clue to the 401(k) fallacy is the ensuing statement in this same quote: "...<u>they used forecasts that were too optimistic</u> <u>to sell the plan</u>..."

Typically, when people are selling or pushing their agenda by using enhanced or embellished data (i.e. too optimistic), someone stands to gain something.

> *Ms. Ghilarducci says she came to realize the 401(k) math she used in the 1980s and 1990s* [when pushing for the plan in Congressional Hearings and Union Meetings] *no longer works.*

Despite misrepresenting sound, or perhaps more reasonable data when pushing the program, she proposes a "fix" to the current problem venue:

> *Ms. Ghilarducci wants to ditch the 401(k) altogether. She and Blackstone Group President Tony James are recommending a <u>mandated</u>, government-run savings system that would be administered by the Social Security Administration and managed by <u>investment professionals</u>.*

So who are Teresa Ghilarducci and Tony James? Ms. Ghilarducci is featured in a New York Times article entitled ***Pushing Aside 401(k)'s for Mandatory Savings Plans***, (Dec. 11, 2015); alongside Tony James, President of Blackstone Group. Who is Blackstone Group?

> *The Blackstone Group L.P. (Blackstone), incorporated on March 12, 2007, is a global alternative asset manager. The Company's alternative asset management businesses include investment vehicles focused on private equity, real estate, hedge fund solutions, non-investment grade credit, secondary funds and other multi-asset class strategies. The Company's*

segments include Private Equity, Real Estate, Hedge Fund Solutions and Credit. [Reuters, Blackstone Group LP (BX)].

This creates a plethora of questions:

1. Hasn't the 401(k) been managed by "professionals" since its inception 40 years ago?
2. Why would this "hedge fund" "professional" be able to create *any* differing result of the 401(k) when the 401(k) rises and falls in step with the stock market, as do hedge funds?
3. How does this "hedge fund" administration propose to keep the market from falling? Are they that powerful, influential, or effective?
4. How and why would the Social Security Administration qualify to administer this program when it is facing its own demise?

Of course these Wall Street hedge fund managers want the retirement money of American workers to be "mandated" to flow into their coffers! Who wouldn't?

Changing the "professionals" is clearly not the solution, because it's not the problem.

The problem is putting retirement dollars on the stock market itself subject to market loss, high fees, and taxes—in juxtaposition to the very popular <u>and</u> common-sense adage: *Do not invest it on the stock market if you can't afford to lose it*. With the odds of the stock market proven to be so horrendous, why would these "professionals" think that *their* investment strategies are the solution, given their admission of using overly optimistic numbers to sell the concept to Congress?

Again, the 401(k) has been a breakeven scenario as reported by the U.S. Federal Treasury from 1992 to 2010 (July 2012 Federal Treasury Newsletter). This is the net result of stock-market corrections, which require long spans of time to regain lost dollars.

> *...401(k) plan has exposed workers to big drops in the stock market and high fees from Wall Street money managers...*

Voila! The real problem in black and white: Big economic drops and high Wall Street manager fees! And yet their proposed solution is to have a *new* set of Wall Street brokers and/or hedge fund managers replace the former ones. How are new managers and brokers supposed to cure "big drops in the Stock Market"?

> *Some early 401(k) backers are now calling for changes that either force employees to save more, or require companies to funnel additional money into their workers' retirement plans...*

Moreover, Greenspan has stood by for decades witnessing the retirement dollars of Americans being squandered and used to simply grease the cogs of the Wall Street machine. Greenspan was easy on his peers, labeling their corruption in 1996 as "irrational exuberance". I prefer more descriptive terms: ineptness, corruption, and greed.

Even with the mountain of scathing reports and evidence of failing pre-tax accounts, the U.S. government, private sector corporations and even establishment radio talk show experts continue to promote this flawed practice: they continue enticing and advising American workers to keep funding these accounts, thereby losing their hard-earned retirement funds. Conditioned by years of this advice, they continue to enroll in these losing pre-tax retirement vehicles.

Financial gurus will counter, "Well, 2001 and 2008 were anomalies. It probably won't happen again." However, the record-breaking streak of 1992 through 2000, spawned by the inventions of computers and the Internet, was also an "anomaly." Yet this windfall "anomaly" was wiped out by the 2001 and 2008 corrective "anomalies". On the stock market, what goes up, comes down—the very nature of the stock market since its inception. On the stock market, *volatility* (ups and downs) is an every-day, every-week, every-month, every-year, and an every-decade occurrence. Thus, by its very nature, one cannot categorize these severe swings as "anomalies." Don't buy the lie.

When you invest on the stock market, your broker or fiduciary representative is supposed to determine whether you are a *sophisticated investor,* or simply an average Joe Schmoe. Typically, your investment endeavor comes with a warning or caveat by which all investors should abide:

Do not invest it on the Stock Market unless you can stand to lose it.

This warning is given because the odds of losing your money are high. If you cannot afford to lose your retirement funds, then they should not be invested in the stock market.

Question: Can you stand to lose your retirement dollars?

If your answer is *no*, then you need to ask yourself the crucial follow-up question:

Why are my retirement dollars on the stock market [e.g. in a 401(k), IRA, 403(b), etc.]?

If your answer to this question is, "Because I don't know what else to do," or "Because I am getting free money with my employer-matching dollars," or "Because everyone else is doing it," then it is indicative of an almost-ambivalent mindset of trusting your employer, his selected administrator, and the failed system. The remaining chapters will push you to rethink these typical responses.

Most Americans are investing, or have invested, the time to attend twelve years of formal education, enabling them to 1) fit into society, and 2) obtain and maintain a steady job. To these ends, many continue this investment of time with an additional 2 to 10 years of higher education, amassing tens of thousands, or even hundreds of thousands of dollars of debt. These Americans will hold these jobs until age 65 or so. After age 65, there are another 30 or more years for which they need to be educated and prepared.

How much time are *you* spending to educate yourself on the crucial funding mechanisms for this 30-year period in which you will most likely be less physically, mentally, and/or technologically qualified when compared to those entering the workforce with new information and/or technology?

Citing the previous Wall Street Journal article:

- *Just 61% of eligible workers are currently saving, and most have never calculated how much they would need to retire comfortably.*
- *People in their 60s who have been socking away money in 401(k)s for multiple decades have average savings of $304,000.*

At $304,000, a $50,000/year disbursement creates only six years of retirement. At that point, unless these individuals have another game plan, they will be reliant on the Social Security payments of no more than $2,500/month. The average Social Security benefit is $1,180.80/month as of 2011.

Both the *solution* and the *education* for this viable solution are available free of charge. I simply ask, for the sake of our economy, that you immerse yourself in this education so that you can go out and compare it to other proposed solutions. Give the third phase of your life the same educational considerations as you did throughout your childhood phase and in your adult academia phase, because neither the pension structure nor the Pre-Tax Structure will cover you.

THE BIG INVESTMENT LIE

When considering a market-based investing strategy, most brokers will advise that if you place your money on the S&P 500 for example, you will average 7% to 8% on your money, as this is the average for this index. This is false. In the Pre-Tax / Tax-Deferred Structure that is invested in the stock market, your money does not perform at the market average.

What most financial "professionals" do not realize is that stock-market funds that are subject to "Loss and Rebound Cycling" never performs at the index average. Just because the S&P 500 has an average performance rate of 7.9%, it does not mean your money will increase by 7.9% annually.

Most professionals will attribute this shortfall to either taxes and/or high administration fees, but in reality, these are not the culprits of the 401(k)'s lackluster performance. Rather, this under performance is caused by *Loss & Rebound Cycling*. For illustration purposes, let's say that the year is 1999, and you have $100,000 in your 401(k). The recession is about to hit, and when it does, the 401(k) experiences three continual years of loss.

Over the course of these three years, the $100,000 retirement account loses 50% of its value, and by 2002 the balance is reduced to $50,000. Here is how it looks:

STOCK MARKET CORRECTION

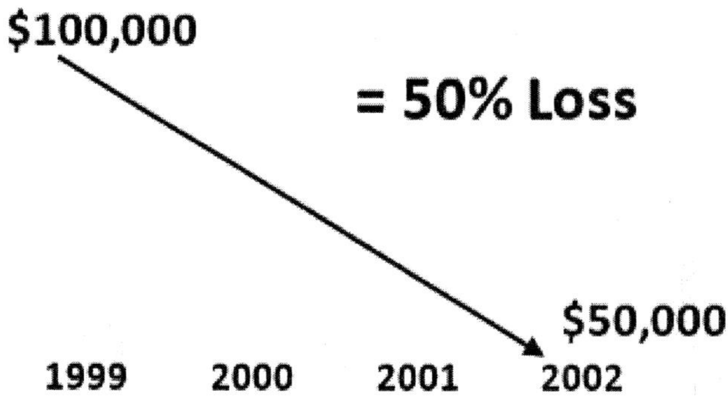

It is at this point that many of the workshop participants, including many CPAs, conclude: *In that we lost 50%, we simply need to make back the 50%.* However, because the money was cut it half, we now have to double our money in order to get from the $50,000 balance, back up to the $100,000 level. In order to *double* our money means we have to make 100% on that money.

LOSS & REBOUND CYCLING

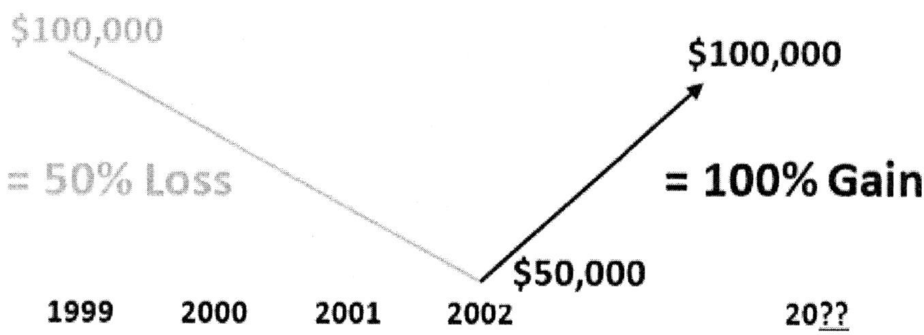

We now need to project how much time is required to double our money, taking us back up to the $100,000 level.

For this, we turn to the traditional formula called *The Rule of 72.* In this formulation, we take 72 and divide it by the interest rate that you are expecting to make. Using the average return 7.9% on the S&P 500 as that rate, and, rounding the 7.9% up to an even 8% (in order to keep the math simple).

RULE OF 72

= 9 Years
8% | 72

Therefore, to double our money (i.e. make the necessary 100% to get from our current balance of $50,000 back up to $100,000) will require 9 years of making 8% on that money, <u>without loss for each of those 9 years.</u> This projection would have looked like this:

2001 LOSS & REBOUND PROJECTION

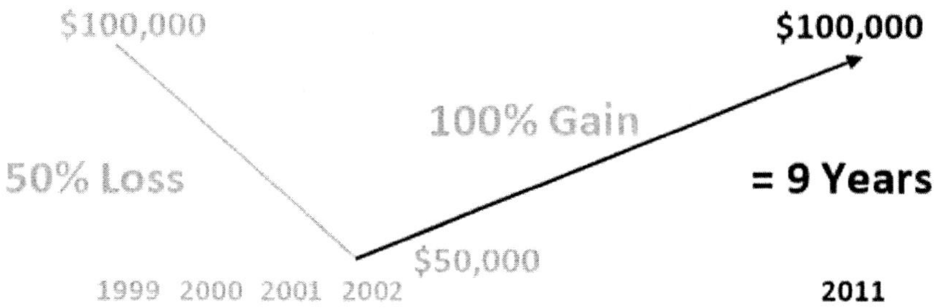

Herein, we see that *if* and/or *when* we make it back to the $100,000, we will have lost 11 years of investment time: eleven years of *lost time*. Unfortunately, the 2011 breakeven point did not come to fruition. While steadily climbing out of our financial pit, we had another economic correction in 2008, which altered our 9-year *Projection Graph.*

2008 DIVERGENCE

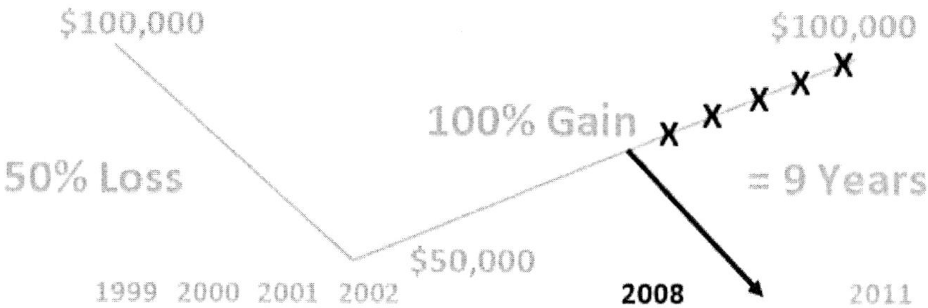

Because of this unfortunate economic downturn, we now have to rerun our *Rule of 72* formula to determine the extent to which our new breakeven date is push back.

2008 LOSS & REBOUND PROJECTION

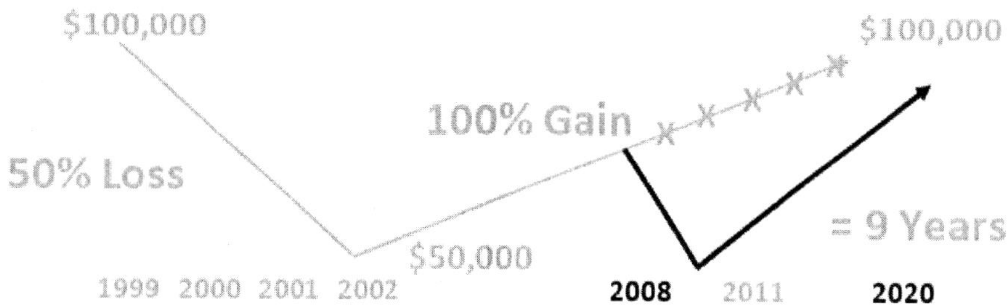

With few exceptions, the actual performance of your money does worse than the index average because of Loss & Rebound Cycling, after which, the admin fees and taxes take their toll on the account. So when brokers tell you that you will "earn the rate of an index's average," for the most part, they are wrong. In addition to this, be aware of the data set on which they are basing their projections (i.e. are they cherry-picking the best numbers to support their sales pitch).

To emphasize the toll that Loss & Rebound Cycling takes on a pre-tax retirement account like the 401(k), let's assess its actual performance on the S&P 500, and compare it to the performance of what I call a *Deferred Income Account* (DIA).

[Side Bar: So that the following comparison us more easily understood, I will briefly describe a few of the attributes of the DIA.

One of these notable attributes is that the DIA is <u>completely removed from Loss & Rebound Cycling</u>—meaning, if the index upon which it is measured drops into negative territory, the account maintains its last highest balance—i.e. it will not lose money. On the downside, it is subject to earning caps, currently ranging from 8% to 14%, depending on the company.

Additionally, when configured properly, the DIA is not subject to taxes (neither the basis or the gains) as this account is funded with post-tax dollars.]

In this comparison, we will begin with a balance of $100K in both accounts, as if the two funds were transferred from previous funds. This data-set begins at the tail end of the booming 90s (on January 1, 1997), includes the recessions of 2001 and 2008, and runs through January 1, 2015.

401(K) VS. DIA

A. End Result (from the original 1997 Balance of $100K)	
401(k)	$211,337
DIA	**$333,439**
B. Gains (Above Original $100K Basis)	
401(k)	$111,337
DIA	**$233,439**
C. Taxes (Based on a 20% Bracket)	
401(k) (on the full $211,337 balance)	$ 42,267
DIA	$ **0**
D. Post-Tax, Net Gains	
401(k) (Net of 20% tax on $211,337)	$ 69,070
DIA	**$233,439**
E. Average Index Performance for 17 Years	
401(k)	6.53%
DIA	**8.15%**

F. Post-Tax, Net Gains Divided by 17 Years

401(k)	$ 4,065
DIA	**$13,731**

G. Annual Return on the $100,000 Investment

401(k)	4.07%
DIA	**13.73%**

The point of this exercise is to illustrate that your money does not perform to the index average when it is subjected to Loss & Rebound Cycling. On the contrary! When your money is removed from Loss & Rebound Cycling, it performs beyond the index average.

IT'S MUCH MORE THAN A PAPER LOSS

Perhaps the Federal Treasury Report regarding the 18 years of lost investment time is starting to make more sense. Relevant to this, in my workshops, I have fielded CPA postulations of: *But this loss is only a paper-loss. They are not really losing this money.*

When it comes to finance, time is money. Case in point: Americans typically work from age 20 to age 65, represented by this timeline:

U.S. INVESTMENT WINDOW OF OPPORTUNITY

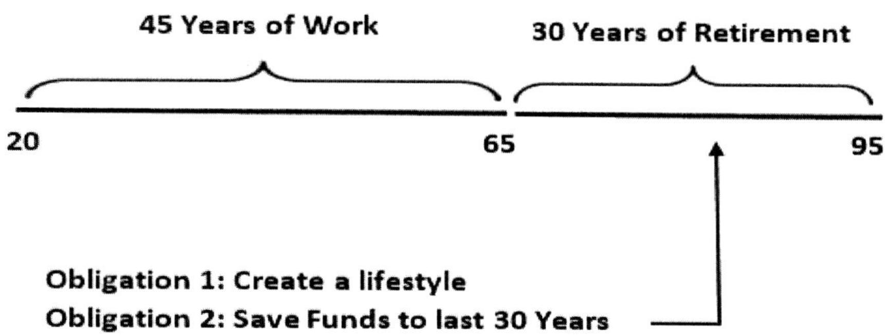

During this window of 45 years, we need to create a lifestyle, while simultaneously putting away enough money to finance that same lifestyle throughout 30+ years of retirement. There are two notable obstacles to this objective:

1. Typically, Americans have been conditioned that we both need and deserve a much greater lifestyle than we can afford. Ergo, retirement is put on the back burner.
2. Most have never acquired the education on how to effectively plan or fund for this vulnerable stage of life.

Additionally, Americans have been misled and conditioned with the following fallacies:

1. You have a pension on which you can rely, which advice has proven devastating to millions of Americans since 1980; or,
2. The 401(k) is a sufficient fix.

INVESTMENT WINDOW OF OPPORTUNITY LOSS

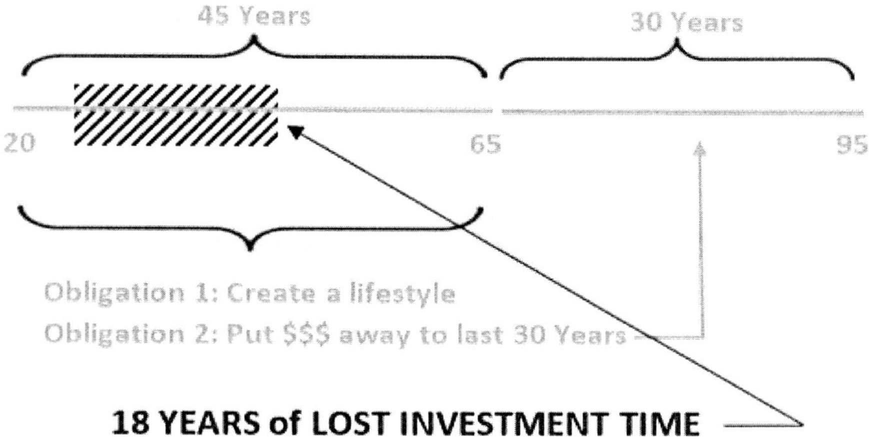

With such misinformation and conditioning, it should not be surprising that we have massive black holes in our investment window of opportunity, which looks like this:

Most people have no idea of this silent devastation affecting their retirement account. The effects typically won't even be felt or realized (and/or appreciated) until 10, 20, perhaps even 30 years down the road when it is too late. Why? Most likely because few entities are interested in educating on these issues. It is not taught in schools at *any* level.

In my experience over 20 years, the majority of consumers themselves have shown very little interest in these issues. Few are interested enough to invest the time necessary to become educated on them.

IN IT FOR THE LONG HAUL

If you are going to participate in a 401(k) or IRA, it is often stipulated that to realize a gain you must be *in it for the long term*. However, what does "long term" really mean? And can everyone really be in the stock market for the long term?

Let's take one of the previous examples and change the numbers to illustrate this *in-it-for-the-long-haul* requirement:

LONG-HAUL FALLACY 1

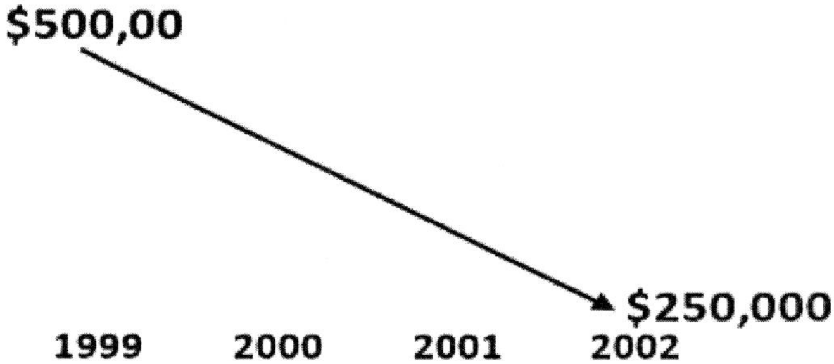

In this scenario, the retiree is 65 years old and, with a 50% slide on the stock market, the account is reduced to $250,000 over the three-year hypothetical downturn. There is one additional problem for which we are not accounting: as a 65-year old *retiree*, he/she is also taking money out of this fund on which to live, during the downturn, while the value of the account is being cut in half. So if this person is disbursing $40,000/year from this account on which to live, the graph would look more like this:

LONG-HAUL FALLACY 2

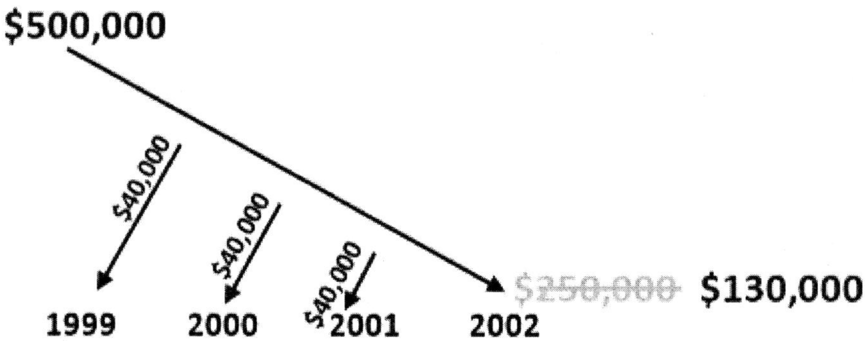

Not only is this client's account reduced by half, but during this slide, he has also been disbursing $120,000 from the account for living expenses. This means that because this retiree is taking funds out on which to live, these funds (the $120,000) will not be available to participate in the upward *rebound*, which scenario was a reality for millions of retirees in both 2001 and 2008.

This person thought he had 12+ years of living expenses tucked away, which has suddenly become 6+ years within a very short 3-year period. IF the retiree's money cannot be in the account for the "upward rebounding gains," because these funds are being used for living expenses, then how does this errant, *long term* tenet apply to this person? Answer: It does not. It cannot. There comes a crucial time for the individual to exit this very risky venue, which we have discovered is long before retirement. Exiting this venue in a wise and timely manner has become a very tricky feat.

For example, let's say this person is 62 years old. He/She still plans to work for another 3 years, and is making $80,000/year. If this person moves the entire $500,000 out of the fully taxable 401(k) in order to move it to a safer venue, then the entire amount ($500,000 plus the $80,000 take-home pay) becomes his earned income for the ensuing year, or $580,000 of annual income. Retirees who attempt this will find themselves in the 45% to 50% tax bracket, and will thus lose ½ of their $500,000 retirement fund—the exact same results as a deep economic correction.

If this person chooses to reduce the risks, and moves the $500,000 to safe investments such as bonds or T-bills, he will experience low-to-no growth on this $500,000 balance, during the period when this person needs big growth on this large balance.

This is the area of estate planning which presents the most significant challenge. How do we move the funds of retired or nearly-retired individuals from the 401(k) to the no-market loss/ non-taxable/ highly-productive DIA, while simultaneously avoiding as much tax liability as possible?

Retirees cannot ever hope to live with any consistent peace of mind knowing that their retirement is riding on the stock market, subject to being cut in half or completely erased without warning. And yet the government offers this vulnerable sector of society no escape route from this tax trap which, by its very nature, comes with extraordinarily high risks—or no growth if you choose the alternative.

There are better ways, and much better vehicles that provide so many more levels of both safety *and* productivity. You simply need to know how to navigate your money from one side to the other. It requires much thought and planning, and is much more effective if you start the transition earlier rather than later.

Bottom line: Because of the entrapping nature of the Pre-Tax/Tax-Deferred Structure, the longer you stay in them, the worse off you will be, and the harder it is to transition out of them—despite the matching dollars, which the enticers label *free money*. In my opinion, this free money is simply a distraction to keep you sufficiently enticed to remain on the sinking ship. When your retirement account is cut in half with a market correction, your "free money" is also cut in half. Regardless of *who* contributed *what,* it is still one-half of what you once had, and more importantly, one-half of the amount on which you were planning.

CHAPTER 4

The Retirement Solution

JUST AS MORTGAGE ACCELERATION is a revolutionary tool for solving the debt crisis that plagues our poor and middle class, so too is the *Deferred Income Account* (DIA).

However, the DIA is much more effective at keeping many more dollars in the hands of consumers than Mortgage Acceleration. Whereas the Mortgage Acceleration concept has created a client-average savings of $164,000 over a 9-year period, the DIA has eclipsed this level of savings. Since its inception, the concept of investment-grade insurance (the basis of the DIA) has prevented the loss of hundreds of millions of dollars that would have normally flowed into Wall Street's black hole.

This concept and structure is a major, life-changing development for the middle class, but only to the extent that the middle-class studies it, understands it, and engages it wisely.

Over the past two decades and after fine tuning the viable redistributive model which eases the debt load of Americans (i.e. Mortgage Acceleration), I then set out to find a consumer-centered retirement strategy that would keep Americans' retirement dollars safeguarded from loss. My criteria boiled down to one question: *What product, system, or approach qualifies as the most productive with the least risk?*

After approximately two years of searching, I discovered a product that met the following criteria. [Always keep in mind that we are comparing these DIA attributes to either your 401(k), IRA, 403(b), annuity, or pension.]

1. No market loss
2. No taxes
3. Contains a Loan Provision
4. High reserve requirements
5. Legally-binding contract
6. Multi-tiered regulation and oversight agencies
7. Flexibility

To achieve *all* of these attributes in a retirement account, we must turn to one of the longest running, cash-rich industries on the planet: the insurance industry. Before delving into each of these attributes, let's first look at the insurance industry.

[Side Bar: When analyzing this solution, you may come to a detail that you do not like, or that you think could be better. If or when you come to an issue like this, I recommend you simply take a step back and ask yourself, "Is this better than my pension or my 401(k) over the long term?" In every case, that answer will be, "It's ten times better!" or, "This doesn't even exist with my 401(k)!" This simple exercise immediately puts things into perspective, and keeps you from going down rabbit holes or chasing red herrings, which Wall Street would continue to have you do.

If, for some reason your answer is "no," then you may find this solution a great diversification or supplement to your retirement. When you put all of your eggs in one basket, your risk goes up, which concept also applies to the DIA. But most Americans don't have the funds to diversify. They're limited to one choice. This being the case, it is time that the public discover a far better choice if they are financially limited to funding just one retirement option.]

First and foremost, these attributes (to date) are only found in the insurance industry. And if the U.S. government were serious or sincere about correcting the retirement crisis in America, they would concentrate on copying the model the insurance industry has had in place for at least 50 years. Moreover, if the insurance industry doesn't want competition, it should step up and fulfill the role to a greater level.

In the realm of life insurance, there are two general categories: *Term* life insurance, and *Cash Value* life insurance, often called *Investment-Grade* life insurance.

Term life insurance can be categorized as the least expensive, and most efficient for achieving various short-term strategies. Term Life is set up for a specific term, after which the policy ends, and there is no cash value for the insured. The insurer and the insured part ways with no obligation to each other. If the insured were to die during the term of the policy, then his/her beneficiaries would receive the specified death benefit, and the transaction ends at that point.

Cash Value or *Investment-Grade* insurance on the other hand has an element of investment included in the policy. In this realm of insurance, there are two major types: *Whole Life* and *Universal Life.* And depending on the insurance company, each of these two branches have seemingly endless options and configurations, each having its own distinct set of pros and cons. I will summarize each very briefly.

Whole Life insurance has been a tremendous investment vehicle for decades. However, in my research and in performing apples-to-apples comparisons to a DIA-based approach to investment-grade insurance, I have not seen a *Whole Life* policy measure up to what I have been doing through these past two decades.

This is not to say, *there is <u>not</u> a Whole Life policy available that competes with this approach.* It's simply that out of all my invitations through the years to produce apples-to-apples comparisons, I have not seen one Whole Life policy yet that competes.

For me personally, the downside to Whole Life insurance is that the company's board of directors (and/or principals) typically decide whether to pay its policyholders dividends each year. If I am counting on this policy for retirement or retirement supplementation, I would prefer that the earnings be stipulated by contract, based on the performance of an index made up of hundreds of companies, wherein 2000+ financial experts determine which companies make the cut. (Such is the case in basing an Indexed Universal Life policy on the S&P 500.)

Moreover, if there is a policy that outperforms my current approach, regardless of its specific strain of insurance, this issue of *discretion of the board* may become less of a drawback. It all comes down to discovering (and playing) the best odds for your investment.

Universal Life insurance comes with a whole host of configurations and variables. From the concept of Universal Life insurance sprang two additional branches or subcategories: *Indexed* Universal Life and *Variable* Universal Life.

Variable Universal Life was quite popular in the late 90s and early 2000s. The *investment* component of the variable universal life (VUL) insurance works in such a manner that the investment or cash-value portion of the policy rides directly on the stock market or indexes. Historically, these policies have been completely subject to market loss. Over the past two decades, many of the ambulance-chasing attorneys have transitioned over to VUL-chasing attorneys. Though the original theory for the VULs was sound, the Great Recession wreaked havoc on it. The *Indexed Universal Life* (IUL) concept addressed and implemented fixes to the VUL flaws and failures.

It is in the IUL where we can see all seven attributes of a viable retirement account (listed on the first page of this chapter), which render it safe, flexible, and extremely productive—more so than anything on the market (to date).

Moreover, the insurance industry is one of the longest established and most successful industries on the planet. It is extremely innovative, and will most likely configure another, more productive investment vehicle in the near future. In any case, its array of products, which includes *Whole Life*, has outlived and outperformed the failed pension structure, as well as the Pre-Tax Structure.

It is also important to know that the IUL product, when used for retirement supplementation, varies dramatically from company to company. This dramatic difference is exacerbated by sales agents and brokers who will write (or configure) each policy much differently than what I recommend.

> [Side Bar: Sales agents have a broad ability to write policies as they see fit. Some policies are written to the benefit of the client/consumer, while some are written to the benefit of the agent, in terms of commissions or compensation. Typically, when there is "fraud" or "errors" with insurance policies, the cause is seldom the insurance company itself, but rather the *agent*. It is for this reason that agents are required by law to carry an "Errors & Omissions" insurance policy to safeguard both the consumer and the insurance company from their errors.]

Additionally, those who oppose using insurance as an investment or retirement-investment purpose typically maintain the general tenet: *An investor should never have to buy something, like an insurance policy, in order to participate in an investment*. To this, I can both quantify and qualify with actual client files, and confidently state that this adage is far from applicable when it comes to a *correctly-configured* IUL, written with the right company. Again, when formulated correctly (with the right companies), nothing currently on the market can compete with the IUL. Conversely, if and when an IUL is not configured properly, this DIA approach (using an IUL) becomes null and void as either a retirement-investment or retirement-diversification approach.

Moreover, and obviously, a well-written *Whole Life* policy will typically outperform a poorly-written IUL policy no differently than two IUL policies written on the same policyholder will have vastly differing results. The following section highlights such a case. Remember: it is always best to get a second opinion when considering this approach as one of your retirement options.

IUL VS. IUL

In July 2014, I received a call from someone who was reading this book. Simultaneously, she and her husband were also in the process of setting up an IUL within the Personal Banking Department at their bank. She asked if I would look at their proposed policy to assess whether it was "configured properly."

The parameters of this IUL were as follows:

Contributions: *$100,000/year for 15 years*

Index Average Growth Rate: *6.83%*

Loan Rate (at Disbursement): *5.8%*

Disbursement Age: *65*

Insured: *44-Years Old*

Death Benefit: ***$5,709,394***

Given the above parameters, this bank-configured IUL would have created an annual cash benefit of $141,728 (based on the chosen index performing at an average of 6.83%).

In creating an apples-to-apples comparison, but with a different IUL company, we were able to configure a $194,894 annual payout—a <u>$53,166/year difference</u>.

In addition to the apples-to-apples comparison, I provided a second opinion, along with a more efficiently configured IUL, advising the couple to structure the policy and contributions differently in order to enable the increased efficiency.

One problem with the bank's configuration was that the policy was only written on the husband, rather than dividing the contributions in half, creating two policies, one for each spouse. In this manner, if one spouse dies, not only does the surviving spouse have the funds available to ease the responsibility of continuing life alone, but that death benefit can also fully fund or finish funding the retirement/investment obligations of the surviving spouse.

Moreover, if the stay-at-home wife/mother dies, the husband is left with having to hire a nanny and/or other help to run his family while he is trying to run his business and fund his retirement. To these ends, I presented that by using the same contribution amounts, they divide the contributions between them, and take out two policies, one on each spouse. In the event of one spouse's death, and with proceeds from the death benefit, the surviving spouse (in this client's case) can continue to fund his/her own tax-free retirement account, with ample money to pay off the mortgage, and continue life as normally as possible. Something as simple as splitting one $5M policy (written on him alone) into two $2.5M individual policies, delivered the peace of mind that they were seeking. And yet this couple wasn't even offered this common sense option. Instead, they were being pressured to sign, therein putting into effect, this poorly configured policy.

By restructuring the policy to better address their needs and stripping out all the superfluous bells and whistles of this insurance policy, the annual payout increased to $312,222/year rather than our original apples-to-apples result of $194,894/year—creating a $117,328/year difference. Comparing the newly and properly-configured $312,222/year payout to the bank's proposed payout created a $170,494/year difference in payout.

This is precisely *why* this approach requires writing the policy to the full benefit of the consumer, and to ensure it by getting a second opinion.

A GENERAL IUL OVERVIEW

To avoid confusion and maintain clarity and academic honesty, it would be beneficial to define the difference between the Deferred Income Account (DIA) and an Indexed Universal Life policy (IUL), which is this: A *DIA* is a properly-configured IUL, configured to the benefit of the consumer. The focus of the DIA is to create a *Life Benefit*, as opposed to acquiring insurance for a *death benefit*. Conversely, an IUL is not a DIA. Remember, a poorly-written IUL can be much worse than a 401(k).

Often while presenting these concepts, when the audience first learns that this approach is insurance based, the body language and/or facial cues are loud and clear: when it comes to insurance, there is a consensus of disapproval.

And as I have said to them countless times in the live workshops, I will say here:

> *Stick with me, I will get you over the proverbial hurdle of insurance's bad rap.*
>
> *Moreover (and paramount), If you want to achieve the 7 Factors of a Safe and Productive Retirement, then currently these attributes only exist in the insurance realm. Additionally, there are more checks and balances in the insurance industry than in the investment industry, relative to market-based pre-tax investment accounts or pensions.*

There are three basic components to insurance-based investment:

INVESTMENT-GRADE INSURANCE COMPONENTS

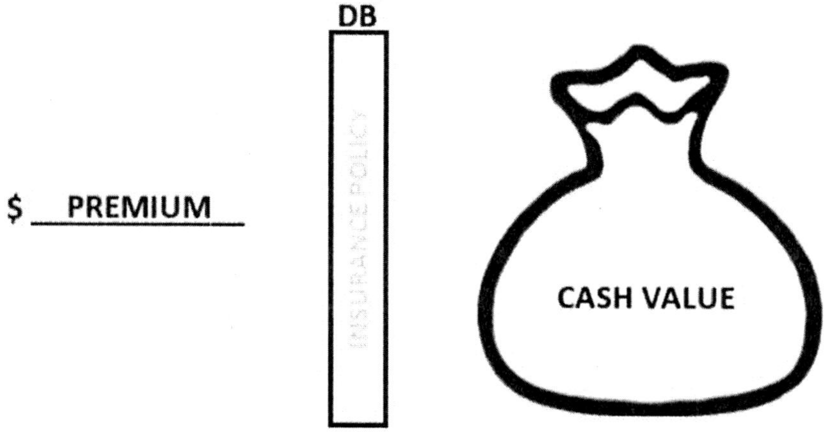

- **Premium:** This is the money paid to the insurance company for the policy and for the cash-value investment.
- **Insurance Policy/Death Benefit (DB)**: The device that covers you financially in the event of death, which also includes a growing investment fund within it.
- **The Cash Value**: This is the residual amount of the premium after your insurance costs/fees are paid. The cash value becomes your investment and/or retirement, depending on your objective.

Now let's play The Insurance Investment Game…

Main Objective: Get as much of your premium as you can into the cash-value bag. But beware, there are three obstacles that can often keep you from achieving this sole objective.

The Play: You cannot avoid these three hurdles. It simply requires that you step carefully around them.

The first hurdle is simple. It is the death benefit. The higher the death benefit, the more money you are using to pay for insurance, and less is available to flow to the cash-value bag. Conversely, the lowest possible death benefit enables the maximum portion of your premium to make its way into the cash-value bag.

HURDLE 1

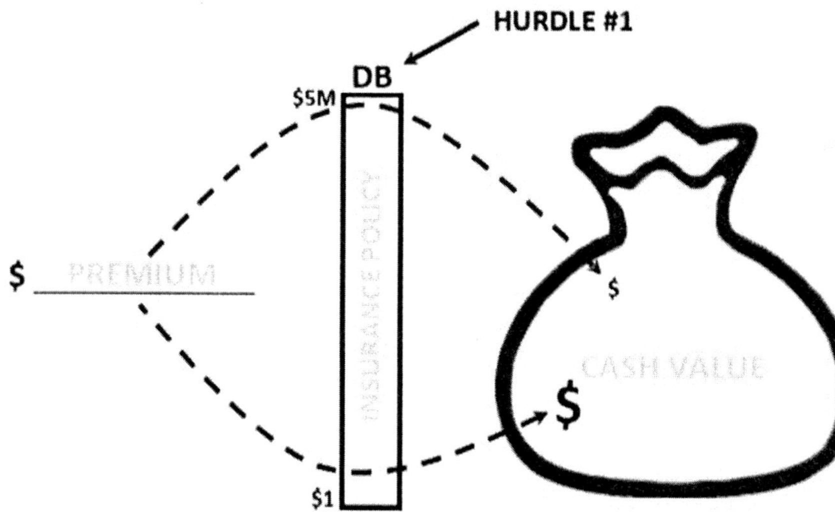

The second hurdle to achieving the main objective is the insurance agent. If there is an error, misrepresentation, or fraud in the life insurance industry it is a very high probability the problem occurred at the insurance-agent level. It is for this purpose that insurance agents are required to not only be licensed; but also required by law and by the insurance company to maintain an active *Errors & Omissions* insurance policy.

HURDLE 2

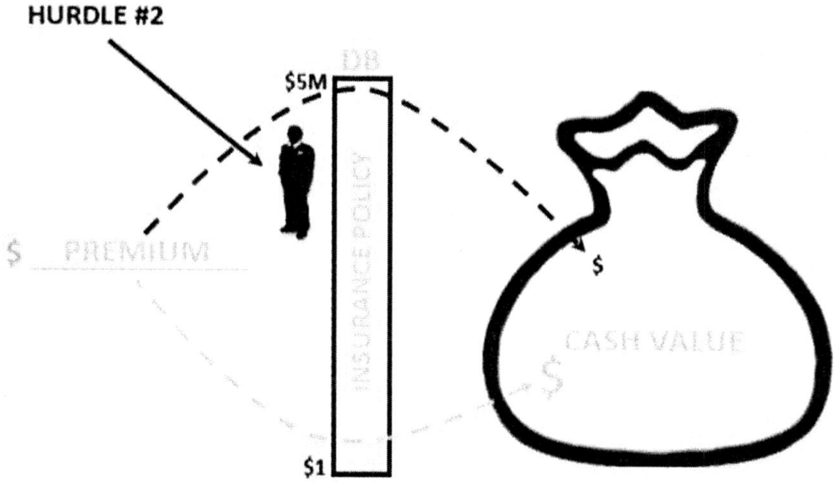

Interestingly, insurance agents receive commissions on the amount of insurance, or death benefit, that they sell, and <u>not on the amount of money that goes into the cash-value bag</u>.

Therefore, they are incentivized to focus on selling as much insurance as possible, rather than engaging in strategies that allow the consumer to get as much of their premium into the cash-value bag for the investment benefit. Once again, we are more interested in the *life benefit* of this investment, rather than "investing in a death benefit."

As a general tenet, you want to go for maximum growth and payout by opting for the least amount of death benefit. If you need more life insurance coverage (above and beyond this investment policy), then simply purchase a *Term Policy* to cover your needs for that specific amount of time until this investment policy grows sufficiently to cover your needs.

HURDLE 3

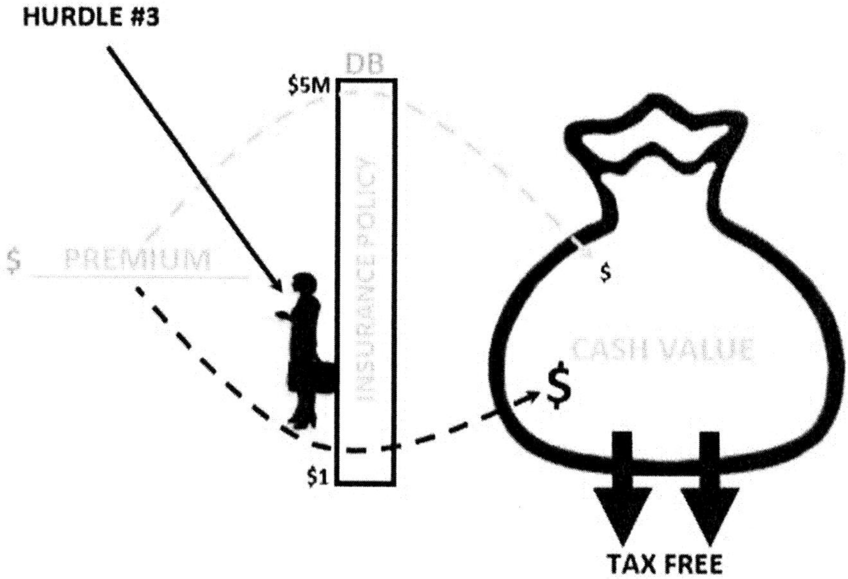

The third and last hurdle to our main objective is the IRS. This agency knows very well how IULs work. In very simple terms: once the money is in the cash-value bag, it all comes out tax free.

In adhering to our maxim: *Minimum death benefit for maximum payout*, I would hypothetically state: *Let's purchase one dollar's worth of insurance, so that $4,999 of our $5,000 premium makes its way into the cash-value bag*. Unfortunately, this option is not possible for the fact that the IRS was well aware of this eventuality, brought on by avid loophole seekers. Therefore, they regulate this approach in the following manner

Using actual numbers: I have a doctor who has been contributing about $7,500/month into his DIA, a dentist who has been contributing $5,000/month, and some young clients contributing $250/month.

For the doctor to get the best return on his investment, he needs to purchase a death benefit of at least $4.735M, while the dentist (contributing $5,000/month in premiums) needs to purchase a $2.545M death benefit. The client contributing $250/month is required to purchase a $539,000 death benefit. In this manner, they are purchasing the least amount of insurance in order to create the maximum tax-free payout.

THE MEC THRESHOLD

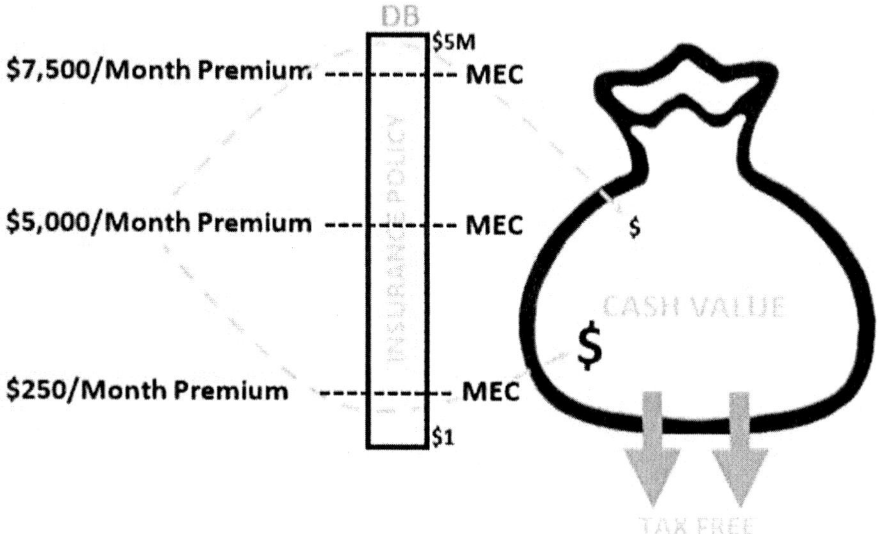

In the case of the dentist, the IRS stipulates exactly how much death benefit he must purchase in order to invest his $5,000/month, which contribution rate he wanted to continue for 13 years for a total of $780,000 in order to maintain the tax-free status of the account.

In summary, this is how the investment game is played in *this* insurance venue.

The minimum death benefit stipulated by the IRS is often called *the MEC level* by those in the industry. The MEC level is the point at which the contract would become taxable. This would occur if the consumer, with complicity of the insurance company, placed more money into the account than what was originally stipulated. If this were to happen, then the contract or policy would be classified as being modified (i.e. modified beyond the limits for which it was originally created). M.E.C. stands for *Modified Endowment Contract.*

Also, the dentist is not required to fund up to the MEC level. If many months pass or, in some cases of an annual-payment scenario, *years* pass without making a payment, it would not unravel the policy. As a matter of fact, after the initial funding period of 10 years in this dentist's case, he will not make another premium payment for the rest of his life.

On the other side of the equation, if the dentist skips payments for a couple of years veering off the original contribution schedule, he has the flexibility and option to make up those payments in future years. His payout will most likely be affected for the simple fact that the insurance company wasn't able to invest his money during those skipped years. And as a result, that loss of investment opportunity for the company *may* result in a lower payout to this dentist, depending on various other factors. This is to be expected, but again, it does not unravel the retirement plan.

What is important to know from this section is that *if configured properly,* this contribution flexibility enables you to fund at a pre-determined pace. Within some general yet wide parameters, you can fall behind on payments, and make them up later (or not), and simply settle for a lower payout. You simply cannot over-fund the account, nor can you increase the rate of funding beyond the originally-projected schedule (i.e. you cannot contribute ahead of schedule). Doing so will "trigger a MEC."

Fortunately, insurance companies keep this from happening. If, for example, a client pays his premium early, the insurance companies will typically contact the clients and inform him, *Your premium will not be applied to your account until the anniversary date of your policy in order to safeguard the contract from becoming a taxable Modified Endowment Contract.*

Lastly, if you know the parameters of the game, keep your eye on the objective, and become proficient on clearing these three hurdles, the IUL cannot be beat in terms of productivity, safety, flexibility, etc.

THE SEVEN ATTRIBUTES OF THE DIA-FORMATTED IUL

To correctly configure the contribution amount(s) and rate of an IUL, we typically use the Debt/Mortgage Accelerator math engine to determine when specific debts and the mortgage are paid off. This gives a more accurate picture of how much money we can free up over a specific period, so that we can form a schedule of gradually-increasing contributions over time.

When coupling the power of the Mortgage Acceleration math engine with the IUL math engine, it forms the most accurate yet simple and common sense approach to retirement planning. It is through this symbiotic relationship between the two math engines that we arrive at what we call the *DIA approach* or a *DIA-formatted IUL*, which we often notate as *DIA/IUL*.

As stated previously, the overriding success of the DIA concept or approach is based on much more than simply finding an insurance agent, and having that agent write you an IUL policy. It must be configured properly and specifically to each client individually, taking into account their overall income, outflow, debt structure, debt payoff projections, their age, their current retirement strategy(s) and/or holdings, and so much more.

Let's look at the seven viable retirement attributes and how they specifically relate to the DIA-formatted IUL.

NO MARKET LOSS

The reason this account is not subject to market loss is because your funds are not invested in the stock market. Instead, the insurance company takes the money in your cash account and invests it in the same things they have been investing in over the past 400 years. However, with a properly-structured IUL the majority of their revenue is made from *Time Value of Money* through the loan provision along with insurance-sales revenue. In short, the insurance company is investing in *you.* [This is made clearer in the *Loan Provision* section in the ensuing chapters.] In this structure, the insurance company's reliance on *investment income* is minimal. When you come to understand this concept (as taught in the workshops), you come to see how it creates a *perpetual retirement fund*, unlike the failing Pension or Pre-Tax constructs, or even Social Security. Government would do well to both study and mimic this structure.

Upon creating your policy, the insurance company offers you a choice: *On which index would you like your cash value to be assessed or rewarded?* Additionally, you can normally opt for a crediting period (i.e. *from* which point *to* which point you opt for them to assess how much your account will be credited), say, from month-to-month, quarter-to-quarter, or year-to-year, just to name a few. Also, the company will have a *Cap* and a *Floor,* which looks like this:

CAP & FLOOR STRUCTURE

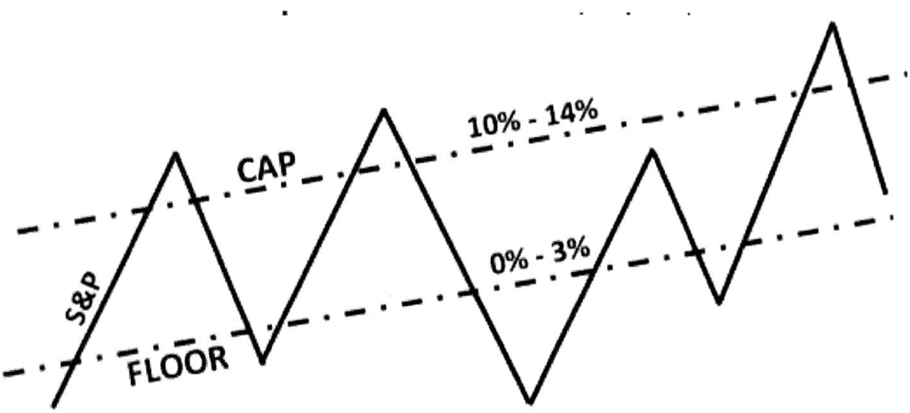

Stock market indices move sporadically up and down, as this is their very nature.

Depending on the company and many factors behind the insurance company's decision, the cap rates have typically ridden between 10% and 14% since the inception of the IUL. In this example, assuming the *cap rate* was 14%: If the S&P 500 performs at 14% or better, you would be capped at a 14% gain on your balance.

ABOVE-CAP LOSSES

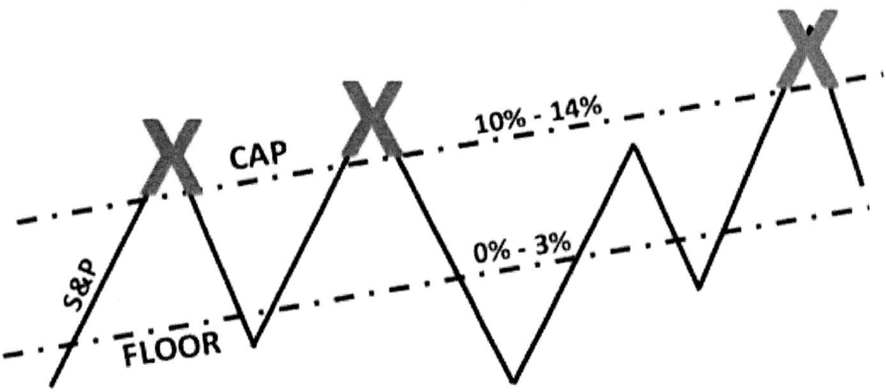

The company may, at any time, raise or lower the cap rate depending on the economy, the health of the company, or other factors. The incentive that safeguards them from lowering the cap rate too drastically, or for too long of a period, is *market competition.* In other words, an insurance company becomes less attractive to new policyholders (i.e. those shopping for these types of policies are looking for high cap rates). If the company isn't making any upward adjustments to the cap rates, policyholders whose policies are completely funded *may* opt to take their funds, or a portion thereof, elsewhere. Sheer competition keeps these cap rates competitive. There is a contractual *Minimum Cap Rate* which the company cannot breach (typically ranging from 4% to 6% depending on the company and the product). This mechanism, or the ability to raise and lower caps, also enables the company to maintain its financial stability.

[Side Bar: Upon stepping into the insurance realm for investment purposes, you will inevitably run into *Whole Life* advocates who will object to IULs because of the IUL companies' ability to raise and lower the cap rate.

Comparing apples-to-apples: Whole Life companies have the ability to withhold dividends from the policyholders in any given year (or years); whereas the IUL provides a contract which states, "If my chosen index performs at a specific rate, then I get a specific amount", especially if that cap rate can't be lowered below, say, 4% to 6%. In all fairness, the two mechanisms are equally geared to enable the company principals of these two insurance strains to react to long-term economic downturns, in order to maintain the company's financial stability. It is sheer competition that keeps the Whole Life companies from withholding dividends too long, as well as the IUL companies from lowering their caps too low or for too long.

That said, I am always open to shift my efforts to forging an effective DIA-formatted *Whole Life* policy, if and/or when the Whole Life industry steps up its game to compete with the DIA-formatted IUL in terms of productivity.

Moreover, in my experience of performing apples-to-apples comparisons between Whole Life and IUL policies, I have found that the Whole Life policies do not produce the robust payouts until the client reaches approximately age 80; whereas the IULs consistently produce higher amounts from age 65. From this, I concluded that Whole Life policies, for the most part, were effective for creating *Convalescing* accounts rather than *Retirement* accounts. Simply put, the IUL provides more money sooner.]

Conversely to the caps, the IUL has a guaranteed *floor*. When the S&P 500 dives into negative territory, your value holds at zero, with the exception of admin fees or insurance costs, thus totally avoiding Loss & Rebound Cycling (explained in the previous chapter). Wherein all gains over the cap are irrelevant, so are the any and all "losses." The account will never lose money due to market correction: it holds at its last highest mark.

FLOOR (LOSS) PROTECTION

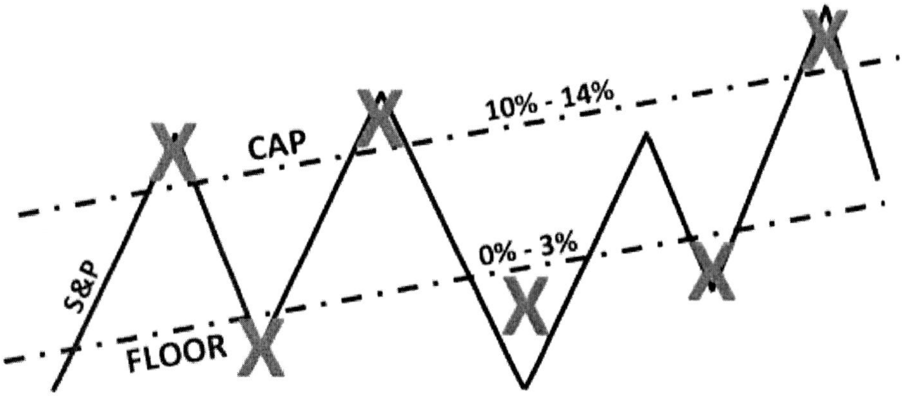

The *floor rate* is also adjustable. While some companies credit you 0%, other companies *may* have a 1% to 3% floor, giving you the impression that if the index falls into negative territory, you would earn that 1% to 3%. Now let's say that the floor rate was at 3%. Often, the floor rate will have a qualifying clause, such as: *We will assess the performance over 8 consecutive years, and if you don't average 3% per year over the 8 years, then we will credit you with a total of 24% over that 8-year period.*

This is *not* the same as, *we will ensure that you get a minimum of 3% every year.* It is much different, and quite trivial and superfluous, because the scenario of eight consecutive years of loss from stock-market downturn has never happened in U.S. history.

The chance of this happening is very slim as the Great Depression constituted only 4 years of consecutive downturn, followed by a 43% gain in the 5th year. Therefore, 8 consecutive years of loss, in order for this 3% *floor rate* to be effective, is highly unlikely for the fact that after the 8 years, everything will be decimated, including the job market, the stock market, the real estate market, and every other market. In reality, you most likely will have been compelled to take your cash value out after the 5th year of loss, simply to stay alive. Again, the "guaranteed floor" rates are *often* meaningless.

If the index you choose performs anywhere between the 0% floor and the 14%-cap, your account balance is credited with that amount.

401(k) VS. IUL

Because various vehicles of the Pre-Tax Structure are subject to Loss & Rebound Cycling, taxes, and to myriad restrictive fines, fees, protocols, and penalties, they simply do not and cannot compete.

In this comparison, to maintain the closest apples-to-apples comparison possible, both accounts, the IUL and 401(k), are considered fully funded or "paid up," each having a $100K cash value in 1997 with no further contributions from that point forward, and no disbursements from 1997 forward. (The assessment of taxes and fees are superfluous in this example: we are only assessing the *Gain and Hold*, no-loss nature of the IUL.)

Also, keep in mind that the percentage in the *IUL %* column reflects the actual cap rates of one specific insurance company, with a floor rate of 0%. Let's round to nearest dollars and put aside taxes and fees. Here is what happens:

1997 – 2015 401(K) VS. IUL

Year	S&P %	401(k) $	IUL %	IUL $
1997	Start	$100,000.00	Start	$100,000.00
1998	27%	$127,000.00	12.5%	$112,500.00
1999	20%	$152,400.00	12.5%	$126,563.00
2000	-10%	$137,160.00	0%	$126,563.00
2001	-13%	$119,329.00	0%	$126,563.00
2002	-23%	$ 91,833.00	0%	$126.563.00
2003	26%	$115,710.00	12.5%	$142,383.00
2004	9%	$126,123.00	9%	$155,197.00
2005	3%	$129,907.00	3%	$159,853.00
2006	14%	$148,094.00	12.5%	$179,835.00
2007	4%	$154,018.00	4.75%*	$188,377.00
2008	-38%	$ 95,491.00	.75%**	$189,790.00
2009	23%	$117,454.00	13.75%	$215,886.00
2010	13%	$132,723.00	13.75%	$245,570.00
2011	.003%	$132.726.00	.753%	$247,419.00
2012	13.4%	$150,511.00	14.15%	$282,429.00
2013	30%	$195,664.00	14.25%	$322,675.00
2014	12.65%	$220,416.00	13.4%	$365,913.00
2015	-2%	$216,008.00	.75%	$368,657.00
Total % **Ann Avg**	109% 6%		138% 7.7%	

*Once the account has been in place for 10 years, this policy gives you a .75% bonus above the index performance (or above the *cap rate* performance).
**Because the *floor rate* is 0%, the IUL is credited with the *10-Year Bonus of .75%*

Often in the workshops, CPAs will quip, *If you subject your retirement fund to these caps, then you miss out on the big gains in each post-correction spike* (as noted in the gray rows in years 2003 and in 2009). However, we are not interested in what happens in any particular year. We are interested in *patterns, over time.*

Even in this small data set, we see two similar patterns, spawned from the same stimuli (the 2001 and 2008 recessions) and yet producing two vastly different outcomes.

For example, at the bottom of the 2001 recession (Year 2002), the balances in these accounts were as follows:

401(k): $91,833.00

DIA/IUL: $126,563.00

In the following year (2003), the performance rates were as follows (keeping in mind that the DIA/IUL is capped):

401(k): 26%

DIA/IUL: 12.5%

We then apply those percentages to the balance of each account, generating gains of:

401(k) at 26%: $23,876.00

DIA/IUL at 12.5%: $15,820.00

Adding these gains to the previous years' balances, the end-of-year 2003 balances are:

401(k) at 26%: $115,710.00

DIA/IUL at 12.5%: $142,838.00

[Side Bar: The above table is configured *without* fees or cost of insurance. That said, it must be noted that over the life of an IUL policy (for a 50-year-old man who lives to age 100), the cost of insurance and admin fees average out to 0.25 percent (1/4 of 1 percent) of the account balance. Whereas, the fees for 401(k) administration typically run between 1% to 1.5% of the balance every year for the life of the account.]

The patterns that should pique your interest are found in the two downturns and severe upswings of the two recessions. Through the 2001 recession, the 401(k) balance slid from $152,400 to $91,833.00, while the DIA/IUL held at $126,563.

Upon rebounding, though the 401(k) enjoyed a robust 26% jump, that high rate of return was assessed on the $91,833 balance. Conversely, though the DIA/IUL was limited to a 12.5% cap, this lower interest rate was assessed on the high-water mark of $126,563.

Pay close attention to the following patterned behavior. By 2007 the 401(k) worked its way back up to its 1999 high-water mark of $152,400, with a balance of $154,018. With the 2008 recession, nearly all of the rebound was lost, taking this account to $95,491.00, very close to the balance after the 2001 slide. In the 2009 rebound, the S&P 500 created a 23% rebound, very close to the 2003 rebound of 26%.

Once again, as a pattern is forming, the 401(k) was credited with 23% on its $95,491.00 balance, while the DIA/IUL was credited with 13.75% on its balance of $189,790.00. After this crediting, the new post-rebound balances of 2009 were:

401(k) at 23%:	$117,454.00
DIA/IUL at 13.75%:	$215,886.00

This pattern illustrates how Loss & Rebound Cycling can ravage stock-market-based accounts. Moreover, it explains and confirms the Federal Treasury assessment of the fruitless results of these accounts.

At the end of this 18-year data set, we have the following account balances:

401(k):	$216,008.00
DIA/IUL:	$368,657.00

Both accounts have been credited or debited according to the dictates of each account, and it's now time to pay the taxes. While the

DIA/IUL is tax free, we assess the 401(k) with 20% tax, arriving at the post-tax balances of these two accounts, which are:

401(k) Post-Tax:	$172,806.00
DIA/IUL:	$368,657.00

For this 18 year-data set, the DIA/IUL outperformed the 401(k) by $195,851 (or $10,881/year). This outperformance, however, means very little in terms of actual retirement provisions—as even the additional $195,851 only creates another 4 years of retirement. Therefore, the greatest attribute of this account that will have more impact on your retirement than anything else, is the *loan provision* (discussed momentarily).

Also in this 18-year data set, the S&P 500 totaled 109%. By dividing this total by 18 years, this index averaged 6% per year. However, in that the 401(k) is a taxable account, that is a hard cost that must be factored in. To do so, we take the post-tax balance of $172,806, and subtract the original balance of 1997 ($100,000), bring us to the net gain of $72,806. In dividing this amount by 18 (years), the annual increase on this $100,000 investment is $4,045; or, just over 4% on the index that performed at 6%. Therefore, as shown in the 401(k) numbers, <u>your money does not perform at the same rate of the index</u>.

The DIA/IUL, wherein we do not have to factor in loss-performance percentages, produced a total of 138% over these same 18 years—based on the *same* index as the 401(k). Dividing this total percentage by 18 gives us an average of 7.7%. Then, by taking the net gain of $268,657 and dividing it by the same 18 years, we arrive at an annualized gain of $14,925. This creates an annual gain of 14.93% annually. Therefore, despite the fact that the index averaged 7.7% during these 18 years, the DIA/IUL averaged 14.93%.

Additionally, by removing taxes from the equation, the DIA/IUL will soar far and above any pre-tax / tax-deferred account. The following section will explain how and why taxes have no bearing on this account.

NO TAXES

The second greatest difference between the 401(k) and DIA/IUL is found in this second attribute: the removal of taxes.

The DIA/IUL is entirely funded with post-tax dollars (i.e. with funds upon which you have already been taxed). Thereafter, the invested dollars (the *basis*) and the *gains* are not subject to taxes when the guidelines of this account are followed. (This will make complete sense after you read the section on *Loan Provisions*.)

Conversely, the basis and gains of the 401(k) are fully taxed as ordinary income.

Any remaining proponents of the 401(k) claim: *You must also account for the tax-deferred benefit of lowering your income, therefore, lowering your taxes on that income.* This would be a valid objection, except for the following issues:

1. The taxes saved from the pre-tax configuration are not flowing into a retirement fund. They are simply reducing your taxes by reducing your income.
2. The contributions to the 401(k) that are reducing your income are creating nothing but lost time, according to

the vast majority of professionals, the government, and news/reporting agencies.

3. Given the fact that the reduced income is doing *nothing* in the current retirement structure, that money could have *at the very least* sat against your mortgage or otherwise improved your lifestyle.
4. The breakeven methodology of "reduction of taxes created by the reduction of income," along with the matching-fund (or free-money) enticements are just that: *enticements* to keep you sending your dollars to the stock market black hole.
5. The complete avoidance of taxes on two or more decades of gains, along with the avoidance of the post-59½ tax trap, and the complete avoidance of Loss & Rebound Cycling far outweigh the meager savings of a pre-tax-reduced paycheck.

To illustrate the loss of the tax reduction through *pre-tax contribution,* let's assess Sam with $60,000 of *gross pay*, and put him in the 20% tax bracket. On this $60,000, he is going to have $12,000 in taxes removed from his gross pay. However, by funding his retirement through the Pre-Tax Structure, that $12,000 tax liability is reduced. Let's say that Sam is contributing $200/month.

At the contribution rate of $200/month ($2,400/year), Sam's income is reduced from $60,000 to $57,600. At the 20% tax rate, his taxes are $11,520.00, a savings of $480/year.

In the previously cited table, the assessment shows that the DIA/IUL created $10,881/year more than the 401(k). The $480/year pre-tax savings created by the Pre-Tax Structure is a drop in the bucket when compared to the tax-free, no-market-loss performance of the DIA/IUL. Worse yet, and more misleading, is the fact that 401(k) proponents will pull out their calculators and offer the following:

> *If you take that $480/year and compound it with interest at X percent, in 30 years you will end up with X millions of dollars.*

This is simply not the case. The reduction of tax dollars is commensurate to the reduction of your income, which is going into the losing and looming tax trap. There is no "extra" $480/year lying around the house: the paycheck was reduced to create the tax reduction.

In other words, paying $200/month ($2,400/year) into the 401(k) in order to obtain a $480/year in tax savings still nets you a zero-gain given the fact that all reporting agencies are telling us that retirement accounts of 2010 had the same value as they did in 1992. *Contributing more money* (as per Teresa Ghilarducci) is hardly the answer! At the end of that proverbial long and winding road, *401(k)ers* are finding themselves in the most hellacious tax trap ever devised. But don't take my word for it. Take the word of those who devised it, and are now condemning it, albeit two decades too late.

Bottom line: Pay the taxes on your entire paycheck. Fund your retirement with post-tax dollars, and (if done within the DIA realm), say good-bye to the IRS for good—both on the basis and on the gains.

THE NON-TAXABLE NATURE OF THE IUL

The reason for the IUL's non-taxable status is simple: because it is a loan—no different than a loan from a bank.

When you take a loan out from the bank, you do not pay taxes on the loan. You must pay interest on the loan...but not taxes. For example, when you take out a $20,000 loan for a car, you pay sales tax on the car, but you do not pay taxes for the $20,000 loan (the loan is not income, it must be paid back).

Likewise, when you take money from an IUL, it too is a loan, and therefore not taxable. Granted! Being a loan, creates a few concerns:

- What is the interest rate on the loan?
- Can the interest rate change?
- When and how is the interest paid back?
- Rather than take a loan, why wouldn't I simply disburse my money without a loan, and avoid paying interest?

The answers to the questions will be thoroughly answered in the ensuing section entitled *Loan Provisions*.

Because there are no taxes due on a loan, the transaction is removed from IRS' jurisdiction and therefore, the disbursements from the account (in the form of a loan) are not claimed as "income." Because they are not income, they are not subject to income tax, and, therefore, this money is not claimed on the IRS Form 1040—or any other IRS form, for that matter.

You do have the option to take the money from your account outside of the loan provision and not pay interest on the loan. In doing so, you would not pay taxes on the basis (i.e. on the original investment or your total contributions), but only on the gains. However, I would highly advise against this for the fact that only by the *loan provision* can you turn a $300,000 account balance at, say, age 65, into $3,000,000 over the ensuing 35 years—without contributing one additional cent, after the funding phase.

Let's take a look at how the loan provision works.

LOAN PROVISION

This third attribute literally saves those who have not been able to put away sufficient funds for retirement. One of the most crucial, timely, and effective aspects of the loan provision is that it doesn't require nearly as much money as a 401(k) or IRA does, to retire. Otherwise stated: you can retire with much less money in a properly-configured IUL than you can with *any* other retirement product on the market.

Let's use a $300,000 401(k) to illustrate the math. If you have $300,000 in a 401(k), and you needed $50,000/year on which to live during retirement, then we could assume that you would have 6 years to live ($300,000 ÷ $50,000 = 6 years).

But how *safe* or accurate is this "assumption"? First, we need to account for taxes. In the 20% tax bracket, the taxes would be $60,000, so you can only count on $240,000 that is yours. We are now down to less than five years of retirement.

What happens if during these five years, there is an economic downturn? If it's not too devastating, you may only lose $10,000, as noted in the previous table between the years of 2014 and 2015 in the 401(k). If however, that downturn is as bad as 2001 or 2008, then a 40% hit would mean your post-tax balance of $240,000 is reduced to approximately $144,000, *less than three years of retirement.*

Solution: Don't use *your* money for your retirement. Instead, let your money continue to "ride" in the same account, enjoying the same gains, while maintaining its complete immunity from market loss. Instead, use the company's money. For the skeptical, this may sound strange or risky, but it is the safest, most secure, most conservative, and most productive option and strategy available. It is the *only* way to multiply your retirement balance (at age 65) by a factor of 10. In other words, turning your retirement fund of $300,000 into a total benefit of $3M, in the case where the retiree lives to age 100.

You literally let *your* money sit in that account for the next 35 years, from age 65 to 100—or longer, and simply take a loan from the company. This would be a good point to return to the unanswered questions we asked at the end of the previous section, regarding the *loan* and the *interest* on that loan.

What is the interest rate on the loan?

For these loans rates, the companies will affix, by contract, an index on which to base the interest, such as the Moody's Corporate Index (MCI), the Libor, etc., the rate at which large corporations in good standing or banks (i.e. with high credit ratings/scores) can obtain loans.

Often there will be a cap or the maximum interest they can charge you during the course of your loan. Currently these loan-rate caps are at about 5.5%. Even if the rates were to reach the caps, as long as the policy is configured properly <u>and</u> your chosen index is averaging the contractually-stipulated index average, you will be fine. Correctly-configured illustrations are illustrated using the loan-rate cap. Therefore, if the illustrated payout works for you, just remember that it is inclusive of the maximum loan rate.

Can the interest rate on the loan change?

Much like the *cap rates*, they cannot be changed for individual policyholders. Instead, such changes must be made across the board, for *all* policyholders. If the insurance company increases its rates too high or for too long, it runs the risk of both losing new business, and/or having its currently policyholders pull funds to invest elsewhere. As these products are continually evolving, be sure to read the fine print.

When and how is the interest paid back?

This is the most beautiful aspect of the *loan provision*: <u>The *loan* and *interest* are not paid back to the company until you die</u>. Again, this may sound funny or odd, but it's true. Each time you take money out from the company, from the day you choose to retire until the day you die, the loans and interest will accumulate, as will your actual funds that are growing for 30 to 40 years, free from market loss.

Your growing fund will act as collateral for your accumulating loans and interest. Don't be afraid or alarmed. The math works out perfectly and the flexibility of disbursements enable you to manage your account and retirement to best match, compensate, or react to fluctuations in the economy, throughout both the funding and disbursement phases.

A few pages back, I illustrated how a $300,000 401(k) would pay for less than 5 years of retirement. Let's compare the behavior of this same $300,000 in a properly configured IUL.

By leaving your $300,000 in the account, with no market-loss and no taxes, and at an 8% average return, over the course of 35 years (from age 65 to age 100), your $300,000 balance will have grown to $4,435,603.29. An 8% projection seems quite "optimistic", <u>but not for accounts that are removed from market loss and taxes</u>.

> [Side Bar: In our actual illustrations, we stay conservative, and typically project between 7% to 7.5% for the index average. However, 8% on your money is still quite conservative, as I have amply illustrated throughout this chapter, as your money does much better than the index average—when taxes and market loss are removed from the equation.]

With your $300,000 fund remaining untouched for 35 years, growing to $4.4M, let's assess how your loan and interest account performs.

The S&P 500's data set for the past 18 years (1992 to 2010), which includes the nation's longest and deepest recessive period in history, produced a 7.7% index average, therein producing an ROI of over

13.37%. Based on this same performance, we should be able to pull out the same $50,000/year, tax free, from age 65 to age 100, and never run out of money. The math looks like this:

Loan: 35 years x $50,000 = $1,750,000.

Interest (compounded): 4.5% for 35 years = $2,508,198.29.

The interest ($2,508,198.29) plus the $50,000 annual loans for 35 years ($1,750,000) = $4,258,198.29. When we subtract this loan and interest amount from our account that has been untouched and growing for 35, we end up with a positive $177,405. This amount would, in effect, become the death benefit and pass on to your beneficiaries if you were to die that year. This previous example, however, is hypothetical. Let's look at an actual client's case.

To create the closest apples-to-apples comparison, it was necessary to split this assessment/comparison into three different phases: the First Funding Phase, Second Funding Phase, and the Disbursement Phase. I began working with this client in 2013. To this point, he had already been contributing into a 401(k) for 11 years (2001 to 2012). He wanted to know how well the IUL would perform during this same period of time had he contributed the money into that, rather than the 401(k).

FIRST FUNDING PHASE (2001 – 2012)

The *Actual* 401(k) Funding (2001 – 2012): This client works for a *Fortune100* financial company.

In 2012, his 401(k) had a balance of $115,587.07. Of this amount, he and his employer contributed a total of $87,400.07, resulting in a total gain of $28,178.00 (or 32.5%) over this 11-year period. This constitutes a 2.93% annual increase on his money. But again, as a pre-tax / tax-deferred account, we still had to assess taxes on the entire amount ($115,587.07). At a 20% tax rate, the taxes would be $23,115.61, which comes close to erasing his $28,178.00 gain. Upon assessing the taxes, this employee's annual return was 0.53% (one-half of 1%).

The DIA/IUL Funding Comparison: Using the same contribution amounts over the same period of time, at the end of the 11-year period this employee's account would have been $119,089.79 (not much over the 401(k) ending balance of $115,587.07).

[Side Bar: The reason for this small difference between the two different account comparisons (compared to the previous comparison) is that this is a new policy wherein the costs and fees are loaded onto the front end of the account.

Keep in mind that costs and fees on the DIA/IUL can be as high as 15% of the original contribution in the first year. This percentage is reduced drastically over the next few years. As explained earlier, this rate will average out to be one-fourth of one percent, whereas the 401(k) administrator fee is typically 1% to 1.5%.

When the *Loan Provision* kicks in, the performance of DIA/IUL will surpass the 401(k) and all similar accounts exponentially.]

Because we cannot predict what will happen on the stock market, we can only use the numbers we have for the previous 11 years, and use them as a basis for projecting the ensuing 11 years. This small data set, 2001-2012, is not very attractive (i.e. two of our deepest recessions occur within this short data set). Unfortunately for this client, it was his reality as an investor.

[Side Bar: In addition to outperforming the 401(k), the IUL also provides this client with a death benefit of $466,374, which was hypothetically effective on Day One of 2001. Should he die on Day One of his policy, his beneficiaries would receive that sum of money. Thus, this vehicle not only outperforms the 401(k), it includes a robust death benefit.]

SECOND FUNDING PHASE (2013 – 2023)

The Projected 401(k) Performance: Using the performance average of the previous 11 years for this account, this account is projected to grow to $264,979.75 by 2023 when this client turns 65 years old.

The Projected IUL Performance: Also, using the performance average of the previous 11 years for this account, this account is projected to grow to $381,468.00.

THE DISBURSEMENT PERIOD PROJECTIONS (2024 – 2059)

[Side Bar: Before comparing these two, it must be noted that from this particular IUL with a $381,468.00 account value, and given the scenario that the S&P continues to average 7.6% through these years (the illustration rate we were using in 2012), then this client will be able to borrow $48,206 each year for 35 years and not run out of money. Because this money is tax-free, in order to create a true apples-to-apples comparison in the disbursement phase, we need to assess how much taxable money it will take to equal the IUL's non-taxable disbursement of $48,206. That figure is $60,258.

Put more simply, in a 20% tax bracket, this client would need to disburse $60,258.00 of taxable income in order to equal our $48,206 non-taxable loan/income.]

The Projected 401(k) Disbursements: By dispersing an annual amount of taxable income $60,258.00 from the 401(k), this client's $264,979.75 account will be depleted in just under five years. In the fifth year, he will have a balance of $45,935—and THAT is if there is not an economic correction during those 4 years.

[Side Bar: Two days after providing this client with this exact analysis, his *Fortune100* bank who administers this *Fortune100* corporation's retirement accounts sent him a statement. The bank informed this client that in order to retire at an income level close to what he was currently making, he would need to begin contributing an additional $4,590.00 per month for the next 10 years, which was more than half of his total paycheck.]

The Projected IUL Disbursements: By taking the $48,206 annual loan (and leaving his $381,468.00 invested in the account for the ensuing 35 years), at age 100 he will have taken out $1,687,210 in loans ($48,206 x 35 years). Given the scenario in which he also dies in this year, his beneficiaries will receive the death benefit of $1,384,020. This is not a printing error. This death benefit is the net result after accounting for and paying back the $1.6M in loans, the interest, and the cost of insurance and fees.

[Side Bar: Throughout the disbursement phase, the death benefit begins to decline until a certain demographical age as determined by the actuarial tables. In this case, by age 78 this client's death benefit was reduced from the original $466,347 amount down to $223,889, its lowest point. From that year forward, it starts to grow again. This is why there is a $1.38M account residual (i.e. death benefit) at age 100 for this client.]

Moreover, it is typically at this point in the workshops that people ask: *How can the insurance company afford to do this, and still stay in business—it seems too good to be true?*

The answer is quite simple: *Time Value of Money*. In this case, the client's money isn't being invested simply from age 40 to age 65, and then trying to live for the ensuing 35 years on that amount. Instead, his/her money is invested from age 40 to age 100—60 years! His money is going to grow to $5M. He will take out tax-free loans which will add up to $1.7M. is insurance costs may reach $100K, the interest for the 35 years of loans will be $1.8M, and result in his death benefit of $1.4M.

If the insurance company is making a steady $1.8M per household over a 35-year period (or $51,428.57 per year per policyholder), it cannot afford NOT to do it. And they have the experience in long-term strategizing and projecting. Remember, some of the companies I would recommend have maneuvered through the World Wars, the Great Depression, etc.

This creates the ultimate win/win for all involved. In *no* venue but insurance can an individual turn a $381,468.00 account into $1.7M in tax-free disbursements in addition to a residual $1.4M death benefit. Having a total contribution level of $166,845 that grew to $381,468, which then morphs into a total benefit of $3.1M at age 100—via the loan-provisions concept: this level of performance cannot currently be accomplished anywhere else but in the insurance realm. During this time, the insurance companies are also making money on both the interest and the insurance.

If there is any *one* industry on the planet that can remedy the retirement crises we are facing, it is the insurance industry. It is also my opinion that this industry is the only contingency which could deter a nationalized retirement. However, the federal government could also mimic this structure and perhaps become profitable. On the other side of the coin, the government has neither the hundreds of years of experience (and therefore expertise), nor the track record, patience, or prowess of the insurance industry (to name just a few attributes).

The last of the questions previously listed regarding the loan provision is:

> *Rather than take a loan, why wouldn't I simply disburse my money without a loan, and avoid paying interest?*

I think this is clear by now, but I will state it anyway:

> *For two reasons: 1) Because if you take your money (outside of a loan provision), your gains on this account are taxable; and 2) your $300,000 balance will be depleted in less than 5 years.*

HIGH RESERVE AMOUNTS

Attribute 4 (of the *seven attributes*) delivers peace of mind that simply does not exist with either a pension or a 401(k).

In the archaic retirement structures, there are no reserves. There is no backup. There is no safety net. If your money is invested in a specific company and the entity goes belly up, such as Enron and myriad others, then your retirement fund is gone. If it is riding on the stock market, and there is a market correction or crash, your money is lost.

Referencing the *Federal Reserve Requirement for Banks* (Chapter 2), which states, "For every dollar in the depositors' cash accounts, the banks must maintain a reserve of about six cents." In life insurance, the reserve amount is approximately $1.12 for every dollar of a policyholder's cash value. This amount varies from state to state, and is normally determined by each state's legislature. What are the protective reserve limits on your pension or 401(k)? Answer: $0!

THE LEGALLY BINDING CONTRACT

Attribute 5 provides a safety factor that delivers peace of mind to the investor.

If you were going to give someone $300,000 over a period of time, and they said they were going to do "such and such" with your money, wouldn't you want that agreement in writing, perhaps a contract? Something which could be enforced should the company not live up to its part of the bargain? *That* is precisely what a life insurance policy is. <u>It's a contract which is enforceable in a court of law.</u>

To give you a better feel for how these vehicles are structured and behave, I am going to summarize the essence of the contract. Very simply and generally, here are the key tenets of these contracts:

- You are going to give the company a certain amount of money over a certain period of time, which you specify.
- You cannot pay more money into the fund than originally declared, nor can you contribute it earlier than scheduled in the *illustration*—a signed document.
- You can be late on your payments as long as there is a sufficient balance to cover the insurance portion of this investment. Late payments *may* affect the loan amounts

(as shown in the illustration), depending on the performance over the years.

For this monetary consideration, the company returns with:

- We will receive and invest your money as we've done throughout our 125- to 400-year history.
- This contribution will also provide you with X amount of life insurance (or death benefit).
- We will credit you based on whatever index you chose, with a cap of X% and a no-loss floor at Y%, which we may raise and lower "across the board, affecting all policyholders equally", depending on the economy. But a reduced cap rate cannot be less than X% (typically at about 4%).
- We will credit you according to the intervals you select.
- If the index you opted for averages X% over the life of this policy, you will have the option and flexibility to take out up to X amount of dollars in the form of a monthly loan, and never run out of money. If the index average is lower or higher than X%, we will inform you of the ideal amount to take out, which will safeguard you from running out of money.
- If you don't need this amount of money in any given year, you are not required to take it. Delaying

disbursements will only increase the amount available in the ensuing years.

- The loan rate is based on a specific index cited in the contract, upon your selection. You may change your index selection (normally at standard intervals like quarterly, semiannually, or annually).
- You may take loans as long as there is sufficient cash value to cover the loan and interest balances, and the policy is not in danger of lapsing.
- You may close your account at any time, but doing so will result in the taxation on all loan amounts, which taxes are payable immediately. Additionally, you will be subject to the listed policy surrender penalties.
- Upon your death, your loan balance and the interest accrued will be repaid by the cash value of your actual funds which were invested (in many cases up to) 60 years earlier. The remainder will pass to your beneficiaries.

This should provide you with the general working knowledge of the IUL. Additionally, you should now realize that other vehicles do not offer this kind of contract/language holding the fiduciary responsible and accountable, while enforceable by law.

Lastly and somewhat crassly to the skeptics: When you lose your 401(k), pension, or investment funds, you're screwed: <u>with a DIA/IUL *contract* in hand, the odds of being screwed decrease significantly</u>.

REGULATION AND OVERSIGHT

Attribute 6 also delivers additional peace of mind, as it, too, increases the security and stability of the account, in comparison to all others.

Insurance is governed by both federal and state laws. Each state has its own Insurance Commission or Department, which sets and enforces the criteria of each type of policy, how it can be presented or sold to the public, what disclaimers must be stated in the sales process, etc. Each insurance company is required to adhere to those state laws and codes.

If there is a question or concern as to the legitimacy of an insurance company, or of suspected fraud, or any other issues, the individual state's insurance commission should be your first contact. In my experience over the past two decades, I have had to call upon these state agencies once, and the results were quick and decisive. They addressed the needs of a handful of clients speedily and effectively.

Additionally, in order to help safeguard the integrity of their industry and keep it healthy, insurance companies participate in a self-regulating organization, which also sets guidelines for monitoring the health of companies within the industry. This organization is called the *National Organization of Life & Health Insurance Guaranty Association* (NOLHGA).

This organization is extremely helpful, proactive, and effective. It lists the history of problem companies: those that were in impairment, or that underwent rehabilitation via the receivership process (carried out by NOLHGA), as well as the companies they dissolved, thereafter transferring the policies (i.e. its cash reserves) to other administrators.

The website is an interesting and informative read. This added level of regulation and safety is found nowhere in the realm of a 401(k).

[Side Bar: The above-mentioned "problem companies" that ran into trouble and were dissolved (as listed on the NOLGHA site) have for the most part been health insurance companies, as opposed to life insurance companies.

Moreover, it is important to note that even "guarantee" agencies can only provide a limited amount of protection, much like the Pension Benefits Guarantee Corp mentioned in Chapter 3. If several insurance companies were to go under all at once, then the Guaranty Corporation would become defunct. However, thanks to the reserve rates of this industry, these accounts will be the last thing standing. But again, it all comes down to playing the best odds and reducing your risk, in an investment vehicle with highest productivity.]

Although life insurance has been around for hundreds of years (more than 400 years for *Aviva*, the first company we used for the DIA-formatted IUL), the industry is also constantly changing. Insurance companies buy up other insurance companies, or companies sell off various departments or products. Therefore, it must also be noted that what used to be a 200-year-old company could also be purchased by a 50-year-old company, thereby erasing those centuries of management expertise overnight. Though such a sale or merger would not affect your policy (or contract) in any way, the procedures and administration styles may be different: for better or worse. Most importantly, the other six attributes of the DIA/IUL far outweigh the high risks and low performance of the 401(k), IRA, etc.

FLEXIBILITY

Attribute 7 of an effective, productive, and safe investment/retirement account is *flexibility.*

Your investment or retirement account should not be so rigid that it cannot bend with the ebb and flow of the economic ups and downs, or from funding errors in either the funding phase or the disbursement phase. Case in point:

I often refer to a 66-year-old client who had $75,000 in her retirement account. Additionally, she had substantial discretionary income which enabled her to fund a DIA/IUL at an aggressive rate of $24,000/year.

To enhance the funding phase, we divided her $75,000 into three equal tranches of $25,000, then added those three portions to her $24,000 contributions for the first three years.

> [Side Bar: At the risk of being redundant, my experience compels me to reiterate that contrary to traditional investing strategies, we do not want to contribute her entire $75,000 IRA funds into the DIA in one lump the first year. Traditional investors scratch their heads at this strategy, because they "think" that with more money in the account sooner, the money will grow faster. Not so!

In *this* case, if we were to move that IRA money into the DIA in one lump sum, the insurance agent's commissions would increase substantially, while the annual payout would decrease. Moreover, the entire $75,000 would be added to her income, resulting a much larger tax bill.]

Additionally, her clinic had a value of approximately $200,000 and, after her projected retirement of 10 years (at age 76), she would be able to sell that real estate. As a result, the last four years of contributions would include four more equal payments of $50,000. Here is what her contribution schedule looked like:

MISSED PAYMENTS CASE FILE

Year	Discretionary Income Contributions	Other Assets Contributions	Total Contributions
1	$24,000	$25,000	$49,000
2	$24,000	$25,000	$49,000
3	$24,000	$25,000	$49,000
4	$24,000		$24,000
5	$24,000		$24,000
6	$24,000		$24,000
7	$24,000		$24,000
8	$24,000		$24,000
9	$24,000		$24,000
10	$24,000		$24,000
11		$50,000	$50,000
12		$50,000	$50,000
13		$50,000	$50,000
14		$50,000	$50,000
Totals	**$240,000**	**$175,000**	**$415,000**

In Years 2 and 3, the account took a turn for the worse because the client forgot to add the two $25,000 payments from the IRA to the IUL. Therefore, the account was in arrears $50,000 for more than two years. This meant that the insurance company did not have the necessary funds "in time" to meet the payouts we projected for her.

I immediately advised her to get the $50,000 in to the company, and prepare for the possibility of having to work another year or two longer than originally projected.

In reviewing her original illustration, we projected for her account balance to be $146,830 at the end of Year 4. Yet after submitting the late contributions, her statement at the end of Year 4 showed a balance of $165,900: $19,070 above the original projection. And this, despite having late payments totaling $100,000 for more than two years. One contributing factor for this unexpected performance was the fact that we project low in these illustrations (under promise, overdeliver). Moreover, she hit her account cap of 14.15% from 2011 to 2012. [Additionally, more good fortune was just around the corner for her again as she hit her cap in the ensuing year, which result is not reflected in this example.]

In continuing with the program, she will be able to withdraw $47,488/year, tax-free, from age 77 until she dies, regardless of the age (given the S&P 500 index continues to produce at the projected average of between 7% and 8%).

This emphasizes the flexible nature of the IUL when it is configured correctly.

As I have already addressed the flexibility of the IUL in other sections of this chapter, I will simply recap the flexible nature:

Flexibility on the front end:

- Because the insurance aspect of the policy is "over-funded," wherein the excess of premiums flows into the cash-value bag, you don't have to make "on time" payments. If you run into financial hard times, chances are the policy would remain effective for years without any contributions. The drawback is that if you skip a few years of premium payments, the projected payout will be affected.

[Side Bar: The worst thing you can do is start a program like this, and then stop funding it in the first few years. I cannot and will not allow clients to start this process until they are financially ready, which readiness takes into account their earning ability, their current debt structure (or projected debt structure), their current assets, and their age. Exceptions to this are those under, say, 30 years old, who will be funding small amounts over a long period of time.]

- You don't have to fund the account up to the MEC level if you do not wish to or are unable. By not funding up to the MEC level your payout will decrease. The only downside to not funding up to the MEC level is that you purchased more insurance (death benefit) than you needed. Again, in this approach to retirement, we are not interested in the *death benefit* per se; instead we are focused on the tax-free *life benefit* of this account.

Flexibility on the back end:

- During the disbursement phase, if there is an economic meltdown, this would also mean that the stock market index on which your IUL is measured is not doing so well. Instead of being credited with 7% or so, you may not be credited with anything, as was the case in 2000, 2001, 2002, 2008, and again in 2015. In these years, especially where it is happening over consecutive years, you have the flexibility to decrease your disbursements, during this slow economic period, thereby allowing for increased disbursements down the road as the economy recovers.
- Lastly, if the index or the crediting interval you choose do not pan out, you can change them periodically.

If you are serious about establishing some level of peace of mind for, and more so during your retirement, then that will require securing a properly-configured account with these seven attributes.

CHAPTER 5

The Symbiotic Relationship Between Mortgage and Retirement

THROUGHOUT THESE PAST TWO DECADES of processing the debt acceleration and the retirement plans of middle-class Americans, I have come to realize the crucial and vital relationship between these two aspects of finance. There is truly a symbiotic relationship between *mortgage acceleration* and the *Deferred Income Account.*

On the surface, most individuals would never see the connection between the mortgage and a retirement account whatsoever. One is a debt, and one is an asset. How would these two products enhance, support, or be *symbiotic* to each other?

Throughout the history of our workshops, I have posed this question: *Is paying off your mortgage before retirement part of your retirement strategy?* The overwhelming response is *yes*.

Therefore, returning to the traditional American window-of-opportunity for financing your retirement, we need to add a third element:

INVESTMENT WINDOW OF OPPORTUNITY LOSS

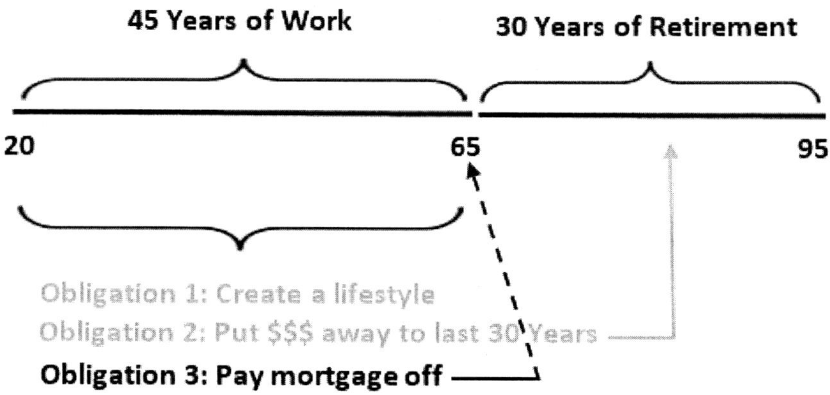

Skeptics will quip that by putting more emphasis on paying off your mortgage rather than funding your retirement, you are losing valuable time necessary to grow your retirement account.

By employing these two formulations in tandem, the possibilities open up dramatically for everyone in all economic classes, especially for those attempting to establish or reestablish themselves financially. If younger people start living these principles earlier, they will reach a much better and more secure financial position much earlier, including the purchasing of a home that they once thought was out of reach.

Moreover, those who have been struggling to get an investment or retirement account funded can now achieve much more in a shorter period, because these accounts are neither subject to market loss, nor to the long delays of "catching up" with the destructive Loss & Rebound Cycling. The efficiency of these accounts is also boosted by the removal of taxes, as well as early-withdrawal or late-withdrawal penalties. Therefore, more money equals less time.

Most Americans have never been educated in striking the balance between managing debt and funding their retirement. To effectively strike that balance, the financial planner must approach the clients' finances in a client-centric manner: each being as unique as a fingerprint. That said, let's look at some general demographic categories, and at the various patterns which emerge.

Generally, for those over the age of 50 with very little put away for retirement, instead of paying the mortgage off in 8 years (under the Mortgage-Accelerator program), we may push the mortgage payoff back to 12 years, enabling them to fund the DIA more aggressively, while having the mortgage paid off in conjunction with retirement. Typically, by pushing the mortgage payoff back 4 years, we may lose, say, $40,000 in mortgage interest to the bank, but we still retained $135,000 of that total interest savings. This $135,000 represents actual funds, which will eventually flow into the DIA.

For the younger demographic that has plenty of time to fund their retirement, and who typically have a substantial debt load, it is best to first ensure that they are in a sound financial position. Such considerations may include establishing a safe position of home equity, removing all consumer debt, and/or establishing backup reserves or on-hand resources to weather an economic storm (i.e. layoff, injury, etc.).

Once the inefficient consumer debts are paid off and substantially more of the household income becomes "discretionary," then we can proceed with retirement funding. We don't even consider starting retirement until clients have established a sound financial foundation via mortgage and debt acceleration techniques.

> [Side Bar: We have a few 18 to 25-year-old clients who are tucking $200/month into these investment/retirement accounts. By age 30, they are increasing the contribution amount to $300/month. By the time they are 65, they are projected to pull out a six digit, tax-free retirement annually. If they experience hardship along the way, they can skip payments for long periods of time. Down the road, they can make up those contributions, postpone their disbursement date, or simply settle for a smaller tax-free disbursement commensurate to the missed contributions.]

For those nearing retirement (with their mortgages paid off), wherein the vast majority of their retirement funds are invested in pre-tax vehicles like the 401(k) or IRA: this particular demographic faces the greatest retirement-planning challenge of all. The 401(k) and IRA are the most formidable tax traps and by far the most detrimental retirement formulations ever devised for this demographic in particular. To qualify this statement, consider this: age 55 to 65 is the period when retirement accounts are, generally, at their highest values. It is during these years where it becomes crucial to have big gains on these high account values! (Exclamation point added for emphasis of this indisputable fact). Yet with a correction equivalent to those of 2001 and 2008, these accounts would instantaneously be cut in half overnight, thereby creating such a huge risk for this group. In simple terms, this demographic is at the doorstep of retirement. In the current system, the ONLY way they can realize large gains at this critical juncture of their lives, is to have these accounts subject to high risks. This is the inherent, faulty nature of the stock-market-based Pre-Tax Structure.

The gurus often tell you to only risk half of it, while parking the other half in low-interest bearing, low risk bonds or CDs, therein defeating the actual value of having these large account balances "working effectively for you", *especially* during the last critical pre-retirement years.

As we learned in the previous chapter, when we lose 50% in a large slide, we need to make 100% just to break even. With historic index performances, this takes about nine years, barring any downturns. If there *is* a correction during those nine years, then that recovery period is dragged out even longer. These individuals will have to remain in the workforce for another decade.

Given the scenario that an individual is 60 years old when he or she experiences the market devastation to the account, retirement for these individuals is pushed out to age 70 or beyond. As long as their retirement dollars are directly tied to the stock market, they will face this ever-present threat and anxiety of delaying their retirement.

The problem, and the best possible solution, comes down to this: in that this group needs high returns on these high-dollar balances, we need to strike the balance between this need for high-dollar returns, while lowering the risk of losing these 401(k) dollars that will eventually be transitioned to the *no-market-risk, non-taxable, highly-productive* Deferred Income Accounts (DIA).

We simply cannot pull out all of the client's 401(k) funds in one year and move them into an IUL because such a disbursement would trigger a massive taxable event. If that account is $300,000.00, then you would be adding that $300,000.00 to your income from that year, putting you in the highest tax bracket. Therefore, it is crucial to follow the S.T.E.P. by step guidelines.

S.T.E.P. BY STEP

The *Strategic Trap Extrication Process* (STEP) is certainly not a one-size-fits-all approach to extricate you from the 401(k) tax trap. In simplest terms, the steps and guidelines are structured so that the taxpayer can quickly, yet cost-effectively transition their money from the high-risk, low-producing Pre-Tax Structure and into the very productive, low-risk venue of the DIA. Moreover, the overriding objective of this tricky transition is to obtain the highest tax-free payout for the lowest contributions, insurance costs, and fees. The trick is to accomplish this task expeditiously enough to get the money into the DIA so that it is growing again at an acceptable rate, while ensuring that rate of transition is carried out timely yet gradually so that the taxpayer can both avoid as much taxation as possible while providing a manner in which these larger-than-normal taxes liabilities can be paid.

[Side Bar: In my years of experience, the most painful time is when my clients begin bleeding their 401(k) accounts, in order to move the money to safer, more fertile ground. To them I simply say, *It's time to bite the bullet.* Uncle Sam has allowed you to defer taxes your entire working life, and now it's time to pay him on both the basis and the gains. It has to be done: get it over with. However, we can keep the pain to a minimum by completing this extraction process gradually, yet effectively.]

For example, if you have $300,000 in your 401(k), you would not want to move it into a DIA in one year. By doing so, your death benefit would increase, and your annual payout scenario would decrease. (Remember, our objective is to get the lowest death benefit, which enables the majority of your "premium," or "contribution," to flow into the cash-value side of the policy. In this scenario, it would be better to contribute $50,000 over 6 years, or $60,000 over 5 years, depending on the age, health, and whatever creates a better payout for each individual.)

Depending on your projected payouts and the state of the economy each year as you near that proverbial retirement runway, we can determine what to do with the remaining $250,000 balance in the 401(k) over the remaining five years (after having moved the first $50,000 tranche into the safer and more productive account).

What you *do not want to do* is to start funding a DIA with the first $50,000 tranche, thereby leaving $250,000 on the stock market, during which there may be a notable economic correction where you lose half of your balance.

If you started funding the DIA with an initial $50,000 contribution from the 401(k), but an economic correction created a loss of $100,000 before we were able to transition it, you would then need to come up with that lost chunk of money to fully fund the plan.

Along this line of reasoning: depending on your age, your 401(k) balance(s), your retirement objectives, and other relevant issues, I often educate clients on moving tax-deferred accounts into a Self-Directed IRA, which is a non-taxable event. This money can then be safely parked into low-yielding CDs or any other low-risk ventures while it is waiting to be transitioned over to the safer, more productive DIA. Within a 3-year period, half of this fund will have been transitioned into the much more productive fund. Though this is not *ideal*, it is currently the safest option.

> [Side Bar: The *ideal* would be to have Congress legislate a provision that would allow this demographic nearing retirement to move their funds into the DIA-type vehicles, assess the taxes at the "date of transfer," and then, perhaps, enable them to pay those taxes over a 5-year period, five years or so after the transfer date. In my estimation, scenarios of this nature would solve this dilemma caused by these tax traps.]

In this scenario, the client will now be adding $50,000 of 401(k) disbursements to his/her annual income each year during the STEP period of six years. This client will be paying substantially more taxes, unless they have substantial write-offs. In reality however, this group typically has its homes paid off. Therefore, this largest write-off (for most taxpayers) is often nonexistent. [Clamp down on that bullet! It's time to pay the piper!] For those further distanced from retirement's doorstep: the sooner you extricate yourself from the Pre-Tax Structure, the less *tax pain* and loss of *investment time* you will experience.

The intention of the government and the champions of the pre-tax accounts was that Americans would stop working between the ages of 62 and 65. With the cessation, they would be in a much lower tax bracket because they would be claiming these retirement funds disbursements as their only income.

However, the lackluster performance of these accounts along with the volatile economy has created the following realities:

1. $300,000 (the average amount in retirement savings for this demographic) is not enough money on which to live from age 65 to age 70, let alone from age 65 to age 95.

2. Because these individuals <u>must</u> continue working, it puts them into a higher tax bracket IF they begin disbursing their 401(k) funds <u>while they are still earning an income</u>.

3. If they decide to postpone their retirement so that they can make more money and let their 401(k) account sit untouched, their 401(k) is at risk due to market correction, unless they park it in a 1% growth, low-risk account. Keep in mind that 1% on a $300,000 account produces $3,000/year, or about one month of living expenses for every year it sits in these low-to-no growth

accounts. In the 20% tax bracket, this $3000/year growth is reduced to $2,400.

Because of this trap, these individuals have three choices:

1. They can stop working long enough to gradually pull funds from the 401(k)—avoiding the higher tax rates.
2. Continue working and let their 401(k) continue sitting in either a high production/high-risk or low-production/low-risk position. Or,
3. Continue working and "bite the bullet" on paying the higher taxes as they gradually begin taking steps to implement STEP. (i.e. transition their funds from the *401(k) High-Risk Tax Trap*, and into the DIA.

With Option 3, you are not only getting your money out of the tax trap and into a safe, highly productive, tax-free account, but you are also now free of the *Age 70½ Penalty* where you are taxed if you don't pull enough of the 401(k) funds out soon enough.

[Side Bar: Most people are aware of the *Age 59½ Early Withdraw Penalty* of the 401(k), which is structured so that if you pull out the 401(k) funds before this age, those funds are subject to a 10% penalty, after which they are taxed as regular income, and this, only if you have the ability to access them "early." In most cases, you are barred from accessing them at all, unless you quit working for that employer.

By contracts, few are aware of the *Age 70½ Minimum-Required Distribution Penalty*, which states that you will be assessed another penalty on top of your regular income tax rates if you don't pull enough of those funds out *before* age *70½*. These two age-based penalties literally create a funnel, into which you are corralled into a position where the government can extract the highest taxes possible from these funds.]

For the demographic that is in retirement (typically age 62 and above); those on a fixed income and whose funds are invested in 401(k)s and IRAs, the solution is a bit more difficult. A general rule of thumb for the Deferred Income Accounts is that they require a 10-year period to mature—only if the selected index continues to perform at about a 7% rate, and again, if the policy is configured properly.

[Side Bar: If 10 years seems too long to establish a viable account, take a moment to compare it to an IRA or 401(k). Under the current system, establishing a viable retirement fund within this period would be an absolute impossibility. Currently, it is only through the tenets of the *loan provision* that the vast majority of Americans could feasibly fund their retirement. Such a provision simply does not exist outside of the insurance realm.]

SAFE EQUITY TRANSITIONING WITH MORTGAGE ACCELERATION ASSISTANCE

The symbiotic relationship between the two financial formulations continues: Remember how after 9 years, the mortgage is now paid off, saving an average of $164,000 in mortgage interest? Well, at the 8-year period when the mortgage payment is no longer sucking $1,800.00/month out of the household budget, that money can now flow to retirement funding. Before these new financial concepts came into being, this same household was going to have to pay the additional mortgage payments for another 21 years. With these payments erased, this windfall of cash can now easily fund an investment or retirement account. Therefore, because of the efficiency of *mortgage acceleration*, the average individual can start funding their retirement earlier, and in most cases, more aggressively.

When comparing these landmark symbiotic formulations to earlier and more popular *niche* financial strategies, the popular approaches of gurus past simply don't hold water. Let's use the popular pre-2008 investment strategy pushed by a nationally-renowned financial guru.

> *Never pay off your home. Instead, obtain an interest-only mortgage; pay the interest only—never paying down the debt. If you pay your mortgage off, you are sitting on a mountain of 'dead equity', which you can't use unless you take a loan out for it.*
>
> *Thereafter, take the difference of the lower mortgage interest-only payment, and invest that*

difference in the stock market—in order to generate interest.

In the 1990s, during the rise of computers and the Internet when everyone was making record money, this concept worked, until 2001 and then more notably in 2008 when it eventually caused the financial ruin for hundreds of thousands (if not millions) of Americans with these interest-only mortgages. As home values started to fall dramatically, the interest-only mortgages were being called due, because the mortgage balances became higher than the actual value of the homes—a phenomenon called *being upside down* in your mortgage.

As a result, those who followed this errant advice of these gurus lost their homes, and/or wasted all of those years of mortgage buydown because they diverted this money to the stock market rather than putting it against their mortgage. In many cases, not only was the investment money lost, but so too were the homes.

With mortgage-acceleration injected into the mix, the investment/retirement game changed dramatically. For the pre-retirement demographic (typically ages 55 to 65), which has its mortgages paid off, the equity in the home is not a mountain of dead or useless equity, but quite the contrary! With a little creativity, while adhering to conservative financial principles, they can use the mortgage acceleration concept to:

1. Safely fund their retirement
2. Implement S.T.E.P. protocols

3. Pay the taxes incurred from the 401(k) disbursements

EQUITY TRANSITIONING YEAR 1

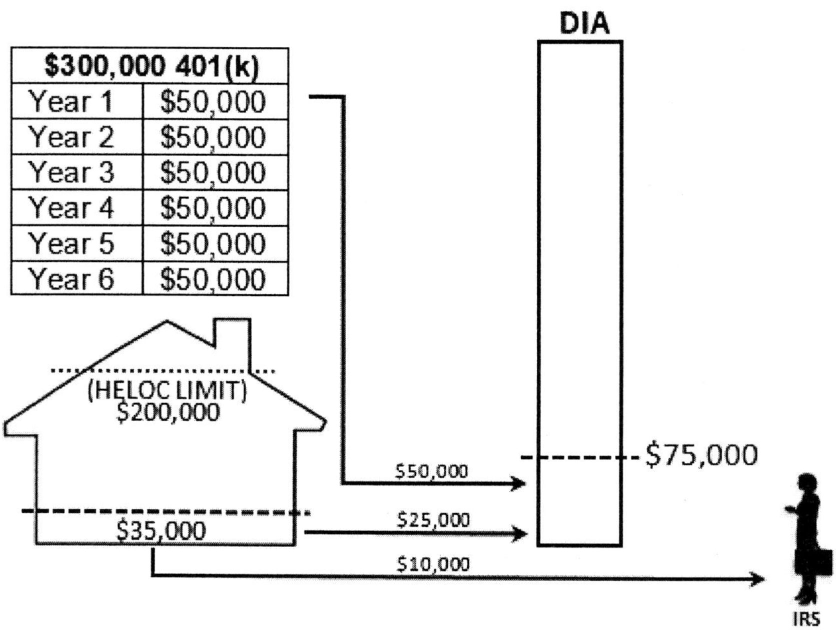

In this example, the $250,000 mortgage is paid off. This consumer has also obtained a HELOC of $200,000.

Because this client is 60 years old, he is no longer subject to the *Pre-59½ Early Withdraw Penalty*, so he can start to slowly bleed his 401(k) into the safe, no-tax, highly-productive DIA as per the STEP guidelines.

Because of this 401(k) disbursement, he will have to pay about $10,000 in taxes each year (the IRS' portion of this tax-deferred account).

However, because he no longer has a mortgage payment, and because he is going to continue working until age 65, this client has a new ability to *also* fund the DIA with discretionary income, to the tune of about $25,000, and pay the $10,000 tax on the 401(k) disbursement each year.

Because his discretionary income is so robust (not having a mortgage payment), and with the ability to place his entire paycheck against his HELOC during most of the month, this individual would:

- take $35,000 from the HELOC
- pay $10,000 to the IRS for the taxes
- add the remaining $25,000 to the $50,000 401(k) disbursement; and thereafter,
- deposit $75,000 into the DIA.

The interest paid on the HELOC is negligible compared to the growth in the DIA, and it allows us to use small, safe portions of their home equity to aggressively fund their retirements, as long as that HELOC is paid back down to $0 each year. To quantify this, consider that the average client (with their mortgage paid off) can pay off a $35,000 HELOC balance with 4% interest in about 9 months. [Keep in mind that the balance is reduced dramatically each month through the mortgage acceleration. Therefore, the HELOC-interest payments total approximately $760 for this period, while $35,000 at 7% in the DIA generates approximately $2,450 interest income. In the following year however, while the cost of transitioning the second tranche of $35,000 remains at $760, we now have a total of $70,000 ($35,000 x 2 years) earning the 7%, thereby generating $4,900. This reflects the same behavior as we experience with the *Account Ratio Arbitrage* concept. Similarly, the annual *interest-payable* HELOC total remains consistently low, while the *interest-generating* capacity of the DIA grows exponentially each year, with the assistance of compounded interest in an account that is removed from market loss and taxation.

Also keep in mind that this $760 annual cost is not only generating more money, it is allowing you to simultaneously finance your tax liability over the course of each year. [As per the two Equity Transitioning Tables in this section, you can see $10,000 of the $35,000 annual HELOC distribution transferring to the IRS.]

In a one-year period of time, this individual has moved $75,000 of his estate ($50,000 from the investment account + $25,000 from home equity) over into the DIA. And yet with the mortgage acceleration concept in play, the HELOC is paid down to a $0 balance each cycle (less than a year in *equity transition* cases). With a $0 balance HELOC, you owe nothing, and the home is not at risk.

EQUITY TRANSITIONING YEAR 2

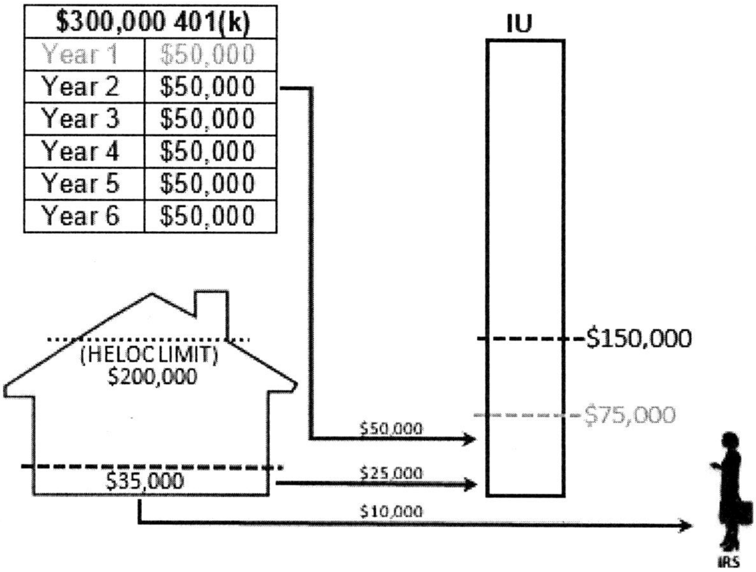

At the end of year two, this client now has $150,000 moved over to the DIA, after which the HELOC balance of $35,000 is once again reduced to a $0 balance. Again, by repeating this cycle for the 6 years prior to his retirement, this client is simply transitioning small, safe units of his home equity, to fund the safe, yet very productive DIA. All the while, he is paying that HELOC down each year through the mortgage accelerator.

Through this slow and steady method, this client maintains a great safety net of $165,000 (the difference between the $35,000 HELOC balance and the $200,000 limit on this HELOC), which is plenty of cushion to stay afloat should something happen during this period. With your home paid off, <u>your equity is not dead</u>! It can be tapped and used in small, conservative, *equity-transitioning* units. Just as with mortgage acceleration, wherein you are temporarily placing your paycheck against your debt (preempting the bank from placing 94% of your cash deposits against *their* debt): you can efficiently fund your retirement using these same vehicles and methods.

> [Side Bar: Instead of contributing to the DIA/IUL in smaller monthly contributions, you can contribute larger sums from the HELOC, which can be paid down quarterly, semi-annually, or even annually with your discretionary income. As the insurance company receives more money sooner, it creates a higher payout. As shown, when STEP is carried out correctly, the interest generated is substantially higher than the interest paid to the HELOC. If it is not, it may be more efficient for the individual to contribute smaller amounts on a *monthly* basis. And yet again, each case is as unique as a fingerprint.]

If you are pressed to get your retirement account funded, and/or if you need a source to pay the taxes on large disbursements from *pre-tax* accounts as we transition those accounts off the stock market, your home equity (via the HELOC) can be employed as an effective tool that will enable you to get Uncle Sam off your back and out of your retirement fund.

> [Side Bar: For the past decade, I have been advising my clients to move funds from their 401(k) and into a Self-Directed IRA (SD-IRA). This is a non-taxable event that puts your 401(k) funds into a checking account, which *you* control. In this

manner, when your premiums for the DIA become due, you simply write the check from the SD-IRA.

The remaining money is parked in cash (or in a CD, or other safe investment of your choosing), awaiting to be transferred into the DIA.

There are several SD-IRA administrators whose fees are a fraction of the typical 401(k) admin fees.]

MATH ENGINE INTERDEPENDENCY

Though the DIA is technically independent of mortgage acceleration, the mortgage acceleration math engine provides the consumer/client with a more accurate picture and detailed plan of how to go about funding retirement proficiently. For most clients, the funding rate cannot be accurately or responsibly determined without a full picture of your financial situation (income, expenses, assets, and liabilities).

Because *contribution amounts* and the *contribution schedule* must be declared upfront in formulating the DIA, the mortgage acceleration math engine proves most valuable in projecting what the conservatively-feasible contributions should be through the years, and even decades, without aiming too high. Referring back to the *Modified Endowment Contract* (MEC), if we project too high a death benefit, and you don't actually fund up to that level, then you are simply buying too much insurance, wherein more of your premium payment is being diverted away from the cash-value side of the account, and into insurance costs. Once we arrive at the contribution amount that you can feasibly afford, we formulate the least amount of insurance that must be purchased to stay under that IRS-specified MEC level.

In structuring the DIA we must establish at the outset the contribution amounts and their intervals. Therefore, it is necessary to project your discretionary income into the future.

Question: *Is it even possible for traditional financial advisors or estate planners to project someone's discretionary income over time?* No. And yet I've been doing it over the past two decades. Let's look at how this is accomplished.

For this example, let's use the Age 30 - 40 demographic, typically married and just a few years into their 30-year mortgage, and likely strapped for cash. They are often racked with consumer and credit-card debt, and child-related expenses, in addition to their mortgage payment. Again, it is nearly impossible to accurately project what each individual's varying contribution amounts should be through the years, let alone through the decades. And *without* the mortgage acceleration math engine, it still is.

Financial planners have typically come up with a solid, round, whole number that "sounded good." And yet as evidenced by the national statistics of the nation's retirement accounts, this traditional "throw a dart at the wall" approach has been a disservice to consumers. Let's look at how we can now accurately project for *variable contributions through the decades* so that we can determine the optimal MEC level for each individual, enabling us to responsibly and comfortably fund a non-taxable, no-market-loss, highly-productive account:

Mr. and Mrs. Smith are both 40 years old. They currently have consumer debt of about $30,000 that is consuming about $1,800 of their monthly income. They also have a mortgage that is consuming about $2,000 per month of that income. Together they have about $200,000 in their 401(k)s, and $40,000 in two different IRAs from previous employers, which they transferred to Self-Directed IRAs, upon leaving those jobs.

Step 1A: IF the Smiths can take a portion of their 401(k) or IRA funds, we *may* want to take $30,000 and apply that money against the consumer debt wherein they are being charged 7% to 20%. This will free up $1,800/month of income and save them $10,000 in interest over the 4 years over which these debts are scheduled to be paid off. At this point, they can feasibly and comfortably start funding their retirement.

Step 1B: If the Smiths cannot take their 401(k) or IRA money, then we would advise using the HELOC to pay off the $30,000 consumer debt, which will reduce their $1,800/month payments down to $125/month, wherein the HELOC has a 5% interest rate. But the difference in payments ($1,800 - $125 = **$1,675**), along with their entire paycheck, will be sitting against and paying down the $30,000 HELOC balance over the course of the year. At which point, we can feasibly start funding the IUL.

Step 2: In that we just freed up $1,800/month in consumer-debt payments, let's use $500/month of this $1,800 to start funding the IUL, and let's allow the remaining $1,300 to flow into the HELOC, which continues to pay the mortgage down at an accelerated rate.

If we decided it was best to go with Step 1A, using $40,000 from the inherently-risky IRA to remove the debt, rather than Step 1B, we would have about $3,600 of residual post-penalty, post-taxes funds, after paying off the $30,000 of consumer debt. Therefore, in the first year of contributions, we *may* want to add that extra $300/month to the $500/month contribution, for a total of $800/month first-year contributions, or nearly $10,000/year.

Let's look at the logic behind using the IRA funds for the elimination of consumer debt:

1. You are removing $30,000 of debt with funds from an account that has failed miserably for decades (as reported by all reporting agencies, including the Federal Treasury).

2. Depending on the terms and other factors of these consumer debts, you could be scheduled to pay $5,000 to $15,000 in interest. Under the logic of *a penny saved is a penny earned*, by saving $5,000 in interest from using your $30,000 IRA (which $30K could feasibly be cut in half with a stock market downturn), you are assuring yourself a substantial return on your money IMMEDIATELY. [*One in the hand* verses *two in the bush*]

3. You instantaneously have $1,800/month in additional discretionary income—which, with this this timely education, you will be spending much more wisely—<u>at</u>

least until you are in a better financial position in your mortgage or in a better position to purchase a home. The latter can happen much faster by following these concepts.

4. Such a move not only enables you to start a safe and productive investment/retirement account sooner, but also removes your money from the tax trap, which becomes ever more restrictive the closer you get to retirement.

The strategies and options are numerous. You simply need to decide what works best for you given your unique circumstances, after obtaining the education and vetting these principles for yourself.

Thus far, the DIA Contribution Schedule looks like this:

Year 1: Pay off Consumer Debt

Year 2: Start Funding the IUL at $500/month

If the Smiths decided to go with Step 1A, and they wanted to add the extra $300/month from the IRA residual rather than putting it toward the accelerated mortgage buy-down, then the schedule looks like this:

Year 1: Pay off Consumer Debt

Year 2: Start Funding the IUL at $800/month

[Side Bar: I often default to a more moderate, conservative projection, rather than an aggressive one, for obvious reasons. A great fallback and flexibility feature is that if we have projected too low, you have the option to postpone the projected retirement date a year of two. Pushing that date back and letting the fund sit untouched for another year or two results in increased disbursement amounts down the road.

That said, in the case where you have come across a windfall of cash or unforeseen resources (say, from inheritance, or bonus, or inherited pension funds, etc.), you *may* opt to live off those funds first, letting the DIA "sit and cook." The longer you can postpone drawing the funds, the more money you can disburse throughout the ensuing years. You may have circumstances which would dictate a different strategy; but these principles and protocols put *you* in the driver's seat with substantially more options.

For example, if during the disbursement phase there is a long, non-productive slide of the stock market, affecting the index on which your account is "measured", you have the ability to reduce the amount of your disbursements from the account, allowing more money to sit unaffected. Thereafter, all of that money will be available to enjoy the large rebound that often accompanies an economic correction. In this case, such a windfall could be tucked away to enable you to pay your living expenses and allow your DIA to sit and grow untouched.

You may wish to simply take half of your projected disbursement amounts at the onset of the disbursement phase, and supplement that amount with said *windfall*, or other funds. Such a move, once again, is equivalent to contributing more money, in that your payouts are increased in ensuing years.]

After the consumer debt is removed, we turn to the mortgage accelerator math engine to project the timeline for having the mortgage paid off. For this example, let's apply our clients' average payoff of 9 years. Therefore, from Year 1 to Year 9, the schedule looks like this:

Year 1: Pay off Consumer Debt

Years 2 - 9: Funding the IUL at $800/month

In Year 10, the point at which the mortgage is paid off, you now have an additional $1,800/month of discretionary income freed up—15 to 20 years earlier than scheduled. At this point, I would typically recommend taking $1,000 of that payment in order to increase your lifestyle, while applying the other $800 to your retirement. The timeline now looks like this:

Year 1: Pay off Consumer Debt

Years 2 - 9: Funding the IUL at $800/month

Years 10-19: Fund the IUL at $1,600/month (or $19,200/year)

At Year 10, the couple is now 50 years old, and, at Year 20, they will be 60 years old. This is important because at Year 20 they will have passed the Pre-*59½ Early Withdraw Penalty* for the 401(k).

Remember, back at age 40, together they had $200,000 in their 401(k). And yet because of the volatility and unpredictability of this account, no one can feasibly project if this $200,000 will grow, lose, or stay the same. Because of this fact, it is impossible to be able to "count on" or "plan for retirement" based on the unpredictable nature of this account, unless, perhaps, it is parked in cash, or a low-risk venue.

For ease of illustration, and in finishing off this sample retirement strategy, we are going to say that Mr. and Mrs. Smith parked their $200,000 in safer, slow-growth vehicles. To maintain our conservative projection, we will assume that their 401(k)/IRA accounts are still hovering at the $200,000 mark at age 60.

In that the Smiths want to retire at age 65, we will divide the $200,000 401(k)/IRA money by six years, which we will round down to $33,000. For the ensuing six years, we will be adding $33,000/year ($2,750/month) to the current $1,600/month contribution level, as we engage the STEP guidelines. The Smith's schedule now looks like this:

Year 1: Pay off Consumer Debt

Years 2 - 9: Funding the IUL at $800/month

Years 10-19: Fund the IUL at $1,600/month (or $19,200/year)

Years 20-25: Fund the IUL at $4,350/month

Over the period of 25 years, the Smiths have paid off their $30,000 consumer debt in the first year, paid off their mortgage in the ninth year, and contributed $591,600 over the course of 25 years into a viable non-taxable account, which has a loan provision. The total contributions look like this:

Years 1-9: $800/month x 12 months x 9 years = $86,400

Years 10-19: $1,600/month x 12 months x 10 years = $192,000

Years 20-25: $4,350/month x 12 months x 6 years = $313,200

With the loan provision, this $591,600 account, based on a properly-configured DIA/IUL, will typically produce a six-digit income throughout the Smiths' retirement years, given the scenario they opt for an index that averages 7%.

If you are still not convinced of the safety and efficiency of this proven, common sense approach to retirement, perhaps you can pose the following questions to your traditional financial planner/advisor:

1. As the majority of my money is in my 401(k), what is the contingency plan if this money is cut in half, or completely lost?
2. In that we will be pulling this money out over the course of the next 20 to 50 years, and since tax rates tend to change drastically over these long periods of time with the ever-changing political landscape: What are the tax rates that I will be facing throughout retirement? If tax rates soar once again as they did in the 1950s, and again in the 1970s, what is the contingency for this?

If retirement planners and specialists cannot project for market loss, nor for Loss & Rebound Cycling, nor for tax increases, then such projections become a mere *shot in the dark.* They are meaningless.

By simply "indexing" your money to a specific index, wherein your money is not actually riding the ups and downs of that particular index, the odds are greatly increased in your favor, while the risks are greatly reduced, and in most cases completely eliminated. The impossible task of projecting for taxes decades into the future is also removed, as we are now operating in a tax-free environment.

With these two symbiotic formulations in place (i.e. a *mortgage-acceleration* and a *DIA-formatted* IUL), the process for arriving at an accurate projection for future finances is the best it has ever been in the history of retirement planning. And given the fact that life is filled with unforeseen expenses, breakdowns, or costly accidents, these tools provide the consumer with far more strategies, flexibility, and options, enabling them to recover from these events and "get back on track" more quickly.

CHAPTER 6

Employers, Employees, and Employee Benefits

AS THE ANECDOTAL ADAGE GOES,

> *You don't cook a frog by placing it in boiling water. Instead, you start with cold water and gradually increase the heat.*

Glancing through the history of employee benefits as an industry, we see how employers have slowly been cooked. Despite the transition of *managerial capitalism* into *finance capitalism* (explained in Chapter 3), the expectations placed upon employers for employee retirements have become too burdensome.

Employers have been slowly, and almost unnoticeably, pushed into the fiduciary role for their employees—the liabilities of which are increasing exponentially as time passes, with three ominous forces working against the employer: 1) Courts siding with employees, 2) Attorney infiltration into employee-benefits litigation, and 3) The failed nature and status of our retirement systems. These three forces have put employers squarely between the proverbial *rock and a hard place.*

Most employers have been led to believe that the failed Pre-Tax / Tax-Deferred Structure is the best (or only) option available for an employee retirement benefit. Now that this structure is proven to be an abject failure, employers are being found culpable and liable for these systemic failures—rather than the experts, politicians, and/or Wall Street gurus who have pushed these wares.

As our law schools are pumping 30,000 to 50,000 new attorneys into the marketplace each year, adding to the 1.4 million already in the workforce, and whereas these attorneys are researching and seeking *new* fields of litigation, and, whereas the U.S. Supreme court recently ruled *unanimously* against both employers and retirement fiduciaries (explained hereafter); these *employer-fiduciaries* are in the crosshairs of these attorneys' scopes. As per the unanimous rulings by the U.S. ju

THE EMPLOYER-FIDUCIARY

As was originally intended, the employer began extending employee benefits, in order to attract and retain high-quality employees. Under managerial capitalism, they offered pensions, which structure proved unsustainable. In the post-pension era (mid-1980s), they replaced the pension with the Pre-Tax Structure (401(k), IRA, etc.). In this transition, employers were required to obtain specifically-trained administrators to manage these accounts.

However, early in this process, administrators were offering perks to these employer-clients in order to attract business, which created a direct conflict of interest. As there was money to be made in the employee benefits industry, entrepreneurial-minded employers were selecting family members, close friends, and/or associates to be the administrator(s) for these accounts—again, creating the same conflict of interest. This new field of litigation has created a new strain of attorneys: *401(k) Chasers*.

By their very nature of investment accounts, these losing 401(k) accounts have a long-lasting paper trail, making it relatively easy for attorneys (and their researchers) to discover these relationships, investment strategies, who selected the administrator, any perks given or exchanged, etc. For example, and referencing the ensuing U.S. Supreme Court cases, if the retirement accounts had above-average losses, above average administration fees, and/or above-average accounting complexities; <u>and</u> the employer showed no signs of moving these accounts to a more profitable, less expensive, or more simplified plan, then the employer can be held negligent or liable—and rightfully so (and this, despite my historic pro-business disposition).

If the employer is actively selecting the administrator, he/she is, in part, acting as fiduciary on behalf of the employee simply by *directing where this money goes* and *by whom it is handled*. Moreover, if the employer does little or nothing to monitor the productivity or trends of these accounts (while in the hands of the fiduciary it has selected to handle these funds), then the employer has some level of liability—just as the courts are finding. When there are kickbacks in the mix, the liability inherent with this *partial-fiduciary* role increases. With continued losses inherent with this structure, affected employees (right or wrong) will be dragging employers into court.

Lastly, employers should not be, nor should they ever have been, put in such a fiduciary role. They do not have the necessary education or training, nor is it anywhere close to their primary focus or purpose: and yet they have now assumed legal and financial responsibility for any hiccups or failures.

As reported by the Bureau of Labor Statistics in 2012, employees are staying with their employer for only 4.4 years, which underscores two relevant conclusions:

1. The original intention of offering an employee benefit to both *attract* and *retain* employees has not served its purpose; and/or
2. As the 401(k) has proven fruitless, it has become irrelevant as a *benefit* in the mind of the American worker, and hardly a determining factor in the decision to stay with an employer.

That said, employers are left with these two sobering questions:

1. Why are they continuing to offer this "benefit", which is clearly not working?
2. Why are employers continuing to put themselves (and their companies) in legal jeopardy by continuing to play <u>any</u> role as a fiduciary, especially in the realm of this failed structure?

LARUE V. DEWOLFF

In 2001-02: Petitioner James LaRue directed his employer's HR Department to make certain investment changes to his account. Larue's request was not implemented, resulting in substantial losses to his retirement fund. LaRue's only remedy was to sue his employer for the losses, along with his legal fees. The U.S. Supreme Court ruling against the employer was *unanimous*.

Just as important and/or detrimental for employers is this: Prior to this case, the law prevented employees from suing employers for these types of issues as *individuals*. Rather, it required the employees to bring the lawsuit as an employee-group. This case (and unanimous ruling) opened the door for individual employees to sue their employers for any infraction (or perceived infraction) regarding their retirement account. In essence, rather than worry about one lawsuit over one individual account or issue; in today's environment, an employer of 100 employees faces 100 potential lawsuits from 100 different employee-plaintiffs, represented by 100+ different attorneys, for 100 different issues. This slippery slope will be played out against employers for decades to come.

In May of 2015, the U.S. Supreme Court once again took a case involving employee benefits.

TIBBLE V. EDISON INTERNATIONAL

In this case, the 401(k) administrator (Edison International) opted to invest the employees' retirement money in venues with higher fees, rather than investing in proven, less-expensive funds that would have favored the employees.

[Side Bar: In most cases, when these counterintuitive or fraudulent investing practices are uncovered, it is typically discovered that the company or its principals are receiving perks or kickbacks of some sort. Or, they simply do not care what is happening with the employees' retirement funds.

With an increased number of attorneys seeking these cases, and, with increased scrutiny and attention on 401(k)s because of their unproductive nature, employers would be wise to not only ensure that their association with their plan administrator is far removed from *personal* or *close* associations, but also to avoid any form of perks or kickbacks. It is simply not worth the risk.

For the benefit of the economy and the middle class, it is my hope that employers begin to dump the Pre-Tax Structure altogether, and remove themselves from *any* and *all* aspects of *employee retirement*. In that company owners are not financial experts (let alone retirement or investment experts); and whereas public education (including higher education) has failed in educating the public and employers in this realm, common sense dictates this very simple question: Why is the onus placed on the employer?]

Edison (the 401(k) administrator) failed in upholding its fiduciary responsibility. Instead of looking after the interest of the employees, it was choosing investment funds that would benefit themselves.

Interestingly, and alarmingly for employers, Edison lost its case under a very rare circumstance. Such an extreme rarity underscores the U.S. Supreme Court's penchant to protect the American worker's retirement. Before its ultimate arrival at the U.S. Supreme Court level, a lower Appellate Court dismissed the case against Edison because Tibbles' claims were filed beyond the six-year statute of limitations. Despite Edison's legal "clearance," the U.S. Supreme Court still heard the case, and ruled on it despite its expired statute. Whereas the ruling was unanimous, it clearly exposes the resolve of the highest judiciary against fiduciaries, including employer-fiduciaries, especially where lost retirements are concerned. Moreover, we can safely assume that throughout the legal proceedings Tibble's legal counsel deposed and subpoenaed the employer in order to expose every nook and cranny of the relationship between the employer and Edison International.

> [Side Bar: Again, it was the DeWolff Human Resource Director, or HR employee, who failed to implement LaRue's retirement-account request, *not* the employers. And yet it is the employer who becomes liable.
>
> Therefore, the legal ramifications of this "benefit" are such that employers need to both micromanage and trust the actions of its HR department, which department employees can and have literally put the company and the employer in legal jeopardy.
>
> More sobering, in the spirit of Tibble v. Edison and given its unanimous ruling by the U.S. Supreme Court, it could legally

be construed that the mere reading of this book *makes an employer aware of better investment and administrative venues than his current 401(k) program,* rendering the employer liable. And yet, just around the proverbial corner there will be something even better—creating a perpetually renewing risk for the employer. It is for this reason that the solution *must include* relinquishing complete control of the fund to the employee.]

Recapping the two sobering questions facing employers:

1. Given the status of these failed retirement structures, why are employers held responsible for the retirement of its employees, especially with an average 4.4-year retention rate?
2. Given the landmark rulings and the failed state of these retirement vehicles, *why are employers continuing to subject themselves to these legal liabilities, typically brought about by errors or omissions of their HR personnel or the company's plan administrators?*

As it is much more natural for employees to be concerned about their own retirement fund; and, in that employees typically have more of vested interest in that fund than the employer: simply direct them to educational resources (such as this book), and allow them to interact with the fiduciary in a much more hands-on and productive manner. In so doing, employers can shed this fiduciary role, thereby offloading the expenses, red tape, and legal liabilities. By relinquishing this burden, employers are free to place new-found time and energy on making the company more competitive, profitable, and successful. In my experience, this *relinquished burden* on employers is a newfound freedom to employees. With mortgage acceleration added to the employee-benefit package (free of charge in most cases), your employees will thank you.

THE NUTS AND BOLTS OF A VIABLE SOLUTION

Whereas the current tax code for the *Pre-Tax Structure* states, "What you give to one, you must give to all," retirement contributions offer no incentive to retain the best of talent, or to incentivize productivity and longevity simply for the fact that everyone must receive the same "benefit," regardless.

However, upon exiting the Pre-Tax Structure, employers can offer *any* bonus or retirement contribution to any *one* employee, or *any* group of employees based on *any* factors they choose, be it based on longevity, productivity, or otherwise. Employer contributions to the DIA/IUL structure is as simple as adding one single line-item to the employee's paycheck, thereby eliminating all the red tape, along with all the IRS bi-monthly, quarterly, and annual reporting requirements. Such a move would most likely reduce the HR departments by 75%, a burden that should not have been placed on companies in the first place—generating a windfall of savings.

The employee, in turn, takes the line-item increase in his/her paycheck, and transacts with the DIA-IUL administrator directly. Upon this transition:

- The company's red tape and bureaucratic reporting requirements are substantially reduced. The employer's retirement contribution (to the employee) becomes a simple payroll expense, tracked by a line-item entry on the paystub.
- The employee takes that money and transacts directly with the insurance company.
- The employer's legal liability in the retirement-benefits realm is eliminated.
- The benefit can be structured by the employer to incentivize production, longevity, or other benefits to the company (i.e. the company is *now* getting what it is paying for).
- In that the employee is directly managing his/her own retirement account, this also alleviates all issues of portability for the employer. When an employee leaves the employer, there is no longer any bureaucracy from COBRA (with its red tape and reporting requirements)—freeing up HR's workload and expenses.

As for the employee:

- The employee is educated on simplified retirement options, which are neither affected by market loss nor taxes.

- The account carries robust death benefits, which cover the employee's dependent-survivors.
- The employee is educated on how to manage a simplified, yet extremely productive retirement account, with ample assistance available for those who would require it. This education includes planning for the best contribution and disbursement strategies given various economic factors.
- With this approach, employers and employees will typically receive financial education, planning, and account administration free of charge.

By removing the employer from the employer-fiduciary role, not only is the legal liability and very expensive bureaucracy dissolved, but also, the employer can now focus on running the company.

It is also crucial to pivot to a dramatically simplified structure so that employees can realistically self-manage. Consider this: in August 2016, several lawsuits were filed against universities by their employees because their retirement plans were far too complicated for the university's staff to understand. Now consider those being sued: Yale, Vanderbilt, Duke, Johns Hopkins, New York University, and Massachusetts Institute of Technology. If these retirement accounts are too complex for the staff members of our prestigious universities, then how could we ever expect employers <u>and</u> employees of much smaller establishments to comprehend these complicated retirement structures?

ADDITIONAL OPTIONS AND STRATEGIES

In that an IUL can be structured to have multiple owners and multiple beneficiaries, the employer can opt to provide the retirement account, be co-owner, and co-beneficiary (up to a designated amount) under the structure of a *key-man* insurance policy. Moreover, it can set the parameters for the employee becoming fully vested in the account based on longevity, productivity, contribution-split, or other factors the company deems necessary to create the desired incentive-inspired result.

Moreover, as these DIA/IULs contain robust death benefits, and as the employer can opt to be part owner of the account (until the employee is fully vested), the employer can also set the parameters of the beneficiary-split, up until the employee is fully vested, after which the employee becomes sole owner of the account, whereupon his family members become the sole beneficiaries. In this manner, if the employee were to pass away, the death benefit could be configured to cover both the employer's expenses for replacing that employee, and inure to the benefit of the employee's surviving spouse, family, or charity.

Contributions, or matching funds, made by the employer on the employees' behalf become an employee expense no differently than they do in the Pre-Tax Structure. More simplified, *whatever you pay, contribute or offer an employee for compensation is considered an Employee Expense, and therefore, deductible as such, reducing gross profits.* This holds true whether it is a matching 401(k) contribution, healthcare contribution, or a matching DIA/IUL contribution.

[Side Bar: In the Pre-Tax Structure, there is a FICA-matching benefit wherein the employer can deduct the FICA-matching contributions on a pre-tax basis. This deduction, however, is miniscule compared to the overwhelming benefits, freedom, and reduced expenses gained by operating outside the IRS' Pre-Tax Structure, wherein government gets its foot in the door to wield its mandates.]

The burdensome Pre-Tax Structure is not a mandatory program. Employers have opted to participate. It is what they were told to do because it was "the only" option.

There are better options that are completely removed from the currently popular time- and money-wasting systems. When structured properly with a mutual benefit in mind, the employer, employee, and the economy wins. Wherein these trillions of retirement dollars are no longer pooling up in a few Wall Street accounts; rather, they are spread across the population: first, into the employees' accounts, and ultimately into the economy. Compare this to the current system where the retirement dollars are not just pooled into a few Wall Street accounts; it is creating a penniless elderly class. Worse yet, these penniless retirees are now dependent on government aid, financed by taxes on the middle class whose retirement accounts are also failing, creating a vicious cycle of individual and systemic ruin.

When employers transition into a system that ultimately benefits themselves and their employees (such as a system like the Deferred

Income Account), *everyone* wins: the employer, the employee, the economy, and all entities affected by the economy.

[Side Bar: There is still one giant hurdle to clear: transitioning entire companies into the system will be a feat, which is why I suggested that government mimics the insurance model, if the insurance industry doesn't step up. It is the only way, short of nationalized retirement, to save us all from the failing Pensions and Social Security System, and thereby alleviate or minimize a devastating Pension Bubble. The problem: Insurance is a finely-tuned instrument, based on finely-balanced actuarial tables (i.e. not too many policies in one place at one time for one demographic). Therefore, implementation of the system (for employers) must be done strategically—not to fool the insurance company, but to maintain this balance. The key lies in the Mortgage/Debt Accelerator as the main component in the employee benefits package, which solves the first half of the retirement equation: paying off debt and mortgage. Remember, we can fund these accounts in one-third the time using one-third the money. Most employees, like most of my clients, can *phase in* to retirement, over a decade or more. Also, we begin by transitioning *Main Street* companies first, from around the country: they who need these redistributive models most.

If there are insurance providers whose actuarial tables will allow for immediate large-company induction, I would welcome your product(s), and gladly share these models.]

CONCLUSION

THESE TWO REDISTRIBUTIVE MODELS (Mortgage/Debt Acceleration and the Deferred Income Account), which have been in place over these past two decades, have created a windfall of benefits, not simply for my clients, but also for the following entities:

The Consumer benefits by paying two-thirds less interest on their mortgage and consumer debts, creating an average interest savings of $164,000 over a 9-year period. This savings of both time and interest creates much opportunity for improving lifestyle, while increasing the ability to fund retirement (or other investments) more aggressively and effectively. These concepts enable individuals of all classes to quickly improve their financial position.

The Employee benefits by getting his/her invested funds off the stock market, and into an account removed from both market loss and taxes. The account is completely portable, and accessible without age-based penalties because the account is removed from Pre-Tax Structure mandates, and from employer control. When factoring in the *Loan*

Provision, an employee can easily create 10 times the income of any traditional retirement account.

The Employer benefits by eliminating risk and liability that comes with the *Employer-Fiduciary* role. By shedding this liability, the employer also sheds the expenses and hassles of the Pre-Tax Structure with its red tape, compliance measures, and its burdensome reports and reporting deadlines. Moreover, the employer can contribute to an employee's retirement in any way, shape, or form; while structuring those contributions to each employee, so that it once again incentivizes productivity, longevity, etc.

The Insurance Company benefits first, by selling more insurance; and second, from the interest charged for the money it loaned throughout the *Loan Provision* years. Though they *win* big, they *provide* big—routinely waiting 30 to 35 years to recoup these substantive gains.

The Common Banker benefits because his or her bank becomes the financial center through which *all* of the consumer/client's money is flowing. This banker will be writing HELOCs as well as mortgages. For those bankers who wish to help create and ride this wave, they would do well to create a streamlined package consisting of a checking account, credit card account, HELOC or CD-Secured Line of Credit (depending on credit score), as well as an optional streamlined refinance of the first mortgage. The interest rates of this "streamlined package" can be higher than average, benefitting the bank, yet not detrimental to the consumer.

The Mortgage Banker benefits by writing many more mortgages. What I have seen through these past two decades of research and development is that clients have been purchasing and then paying off a second or third home to create a supplemental source of income—in under 15 years. This process is only possible with the mortgage acceleration product. The more mortgages written (in a shorter period of time), and/or mortgages rewritten for strategic refinancing purposes, the more fees and revenue are generated for this banking sector.

The Economy is probably the greatest beneficiary of all. With these vast sums of money being diverted away from the stagnant pools of Wall Street, big banks, and the *One Percenters*, the money finds its way back into the economy quickly and efficiently. Bottom Line: When the economy is healthy and growing, EVERY individual and entity thrives; the rich and the poor, big business and small business, as well as governments on the federal and local levels. Most importantly, this not only stabilizes the middle class: it strengthens it. In this new structure, this demographic is keeping and spending more of its money.

The Political Left benefits because both the middle class and those living below *poverty level* have a much greater opportunity to quickly improve their status. By removing the "retirement responsibility" (and much of this needless expense) from businesses, the business sector can afford more taxes that flow to local and state governments, creating more revenue for social care and outreach programs. Moreover, with more money flowing to the *middle class*, it also tends to donate more to these worthy causes.

The Political Right benefits because these redistributive models are providing the timely, life-saving, and life-sustaining CPR to what "used to be" a robustly *independent* middle class. The political right claims to be the champion of the small, independent businessmen, and America's entrepreneurial spirit (which can only thrive in a healthy, independent, decentralized structure). With the centralized control of industries by a handful of megacorporations, our free market economy is headed the way of large, centralized government: stagnant gridlock.

Wall Street benefits for the simple fact that the economy is booming. The millions upon millions of people with more money in their hands will not only be purchasing products and services from publicly-traded companies, but these masses will also have substantially more discretionary income with which they invest—but only *after* having their retirements safely funded, away from its reach and influence.

In conclusion, as free-market-based wealth redistribution is proven to benefit all entities, market segments, and the economy as a whole. Everyone (individual consumers to industry and government leaders) should be embracing and pushing these concepts forward. It is a wealth-redistribution philosophy in which all can participate and win.

THE VALUE OF REDISTRIBUTIVE MODELS

When *moderately-disruptive redistributive models* are efficiently thought through at a *proficient planning table* so that they are structured to benefit the masses, these models often produce even greater or longer-lasting benefits that are seldom identifiable on the surface.

Therefore, rather than summarily dismissing these often-misunderstood models as foreign or invasive, think past the short-term effects on *your* smaller tribe, and lean toward what benefits the greater good. Given the economic imbalance and income disparity, pretty much anything that brings about a natural, or what I call a *free-market* redistribution, is a good thing. It is what capitalism *should have been* about, as opposed to the more exclusive, elitist, and errant *finance capitalism*.

Examples of this type of disruption are found in Airbnb or Uber; and yet on another level, I've seen a few grocery co-ops and network marketing firms whose objectives are to create a redistributive element within their structure: some accomplish it, some do not (*greed* most often being the derailing element).

One of the most formidable examples of an effective redistributive model, which has produced (and is currently producing) progressive, innovative changes on many levels is Airbnb. On the surface, people see the Airbnb concept as simply a *redistribution-of-wealth* model, when if fact, the potential is much greater.

> [Side Bar: My business partner and I have implemented the redistributive Airbnb model, creating an additional $30,000/year income at a time when funds were scarce, yet R&D and market-testing expenses were plentiful. These extra funds enabled us to make ends meet while getting these financial concepts to market. Therefore, with the *butterfly effect* in mind, the Airbnb model is having a much greater impact on so many lives and sectors (beyond what it has done

for me, or what its contribution to my efforts will have in the big picture). Regardless, it has created huge upside potential in the *ecological* arena (i.e. saving the earth's resources).]

From my experience here in the San Francisco Bay Area, it is typically unions and the political left who find the Airbnb model too disruptive because, on the surface, it appears to be reducing the housing market for the poor and middle class. On the political right, the hotel and entertainment lobbyists fear this level of disruption because of sheer competition. Airbnb, alone, is the cause of billions of dollars being diverted away from the large hotel chains (i.e. Wall Street), and into the accounts of middle-class homeowners, like me. However, there are even greater efficiencies being realized in terms of job-creation and as mentioned, *resource conservation*.

As unions have aligned themselves over the years with the eco/green movement (which concept I support), their primary focus has been to protect jobs and the wage levels for those jobs (which I also support to a point). On the flipside of that coin however, historically, jobs are intrinsically tied to resource consumption. Therefore, ecologically speaking, perhaps our unions should become part of the process of rethinking and redefining the workweek, the workplace, and even work itself—as my associates and I have been doing for years. The dynamic Airbnb model however, pegs three of these proverbial birds with one stone. [Put on your seatbelt!]

In the United States alone, there are about five million hotel rooms in an industry that has historically experienced a 50% vacancy rate. This can easily be construed that there are 2.5 million constructed, fully-furnished and decorated rooms that are unused at any given point. That's a hell-of-a-lot of wasted resources—*double* what is actually required. (Yes, yes, Mr. Union President, I realize that each of those 2.5 million idle rooms also created a hell-of-a-lot of "jobs"; from contractors to carpet makers to interior designers to coffee-machine makers to mattress and linen manufacturers, etc.). But the ecological costs in terms of resources for this unused space are enormous and needless (i.e. wasteful). [Keep your seatbelts on, and your underwear from getting in a knot: the jobs are not lost; they're simply in *transition*.]

In essence, Airbnb, Inc. has creatively found a way to plug "traveling consumers" into existing spaces filled with previously-allocated resources (furnishings, appliances, decorations, etc.): we don't need more. Save the resources for something more needful. The Airbnb concept brings a cornucopia of additional benefits:

- **A massive redistribution of wealth back to the middle class**
- **A free-market forced *conservation of resources*.** As billions of dollars are now being diverted away from the resource-gluttonous hotel industry (by *dollar vote* of the consumer), it forces the industry to change not only its business model, but also its resource-consumption model. It can no longer afford to purchase double the resources in order to build *double its occupancy requirement*. The hotel industry may counter with a viable reason for needing the idle rooms; such as for peak-season demand. However, Airbnb can fill this demand more

efficiently in terms of *resource usage*. More importantly and the main objective in using Airbnb as the example is to emphasize better time, money, energy, and resource allocation in *all* industries. This is what redistributive modeling is about; or, at least, *should be* about.

To further this ecological trend, environmentally-minded consumers should consider staying at hotels/motels that are mindful of this new concept (i.e. those entities that have downsized or who have figured a way to improve their vacancy rates, therein managing *our collective resources* more wisely. Or, consumers continue booking at Airbnb. Most importantly, like-minded citizens should vote to block local measures that hinder these sound, progressive, and much more efficient models.

- **A most-plausible solution to the housing shortage**. As many of these hotels will find it more difficult to compete, they will eventually downsize, or go out of business. As the least-efficient hotel chains go under, capitalism (and/or the government) steps in to make lemonade out of the bounteous lemons. As this transformation takes place (in order to compete with Airbnb's more efficient model), the inefficient chains will begin to sell off assets (i.e. high-rise hotels and motels). Government and entrepreneurs can purchase these units and convert them into medium- and high-density housing (ding-ding-ding-ding-ding....JOBS), <u>with resources that have</u>

already been allocated to that existing space. This is *better* than recycling.

As the financially-unprepared baby-boomers enter retirement, the government needs affordable places to house these people—rather than leaving them homeless, or increasing taxes to create new spaces for them (requiring even more raw material and resources).

- **Transitioned jobs.** To the *jobs*-minded entities (unions), these hotels and motels will need retrofitting and remodeling—creating jobs. People will need new mattresses, linens, and other furnishings—which maintains (without disrupting) those manufacturing jobs. These units will need ongoing management, therein transitioning the service-industry jobs to property-maintenance and management jobs. Many of these structures already have large kitchens and cafeteria space, which would serve the convalescent demographic perfectly.

  In short, these jobs are not lost: simply *transitioned.*

What is our alternative? Status quo? Continue using double the resources (than necessary) in our industries, as if we have an endless supply? *Drill baby! Drill! It doesn't matter how much or how fast we use the resources: God is coming to save me and my tribe anyway*?

[Side Bar: My citing of these status quo mindsets is not to disrespect any particular demographic or religious belief, but instead to make this point: This clear, present, and very popular behavior resulting from these worrisome mindsets affects the future of us all, (including other spiritually-minded and non-spiritually-minded individuals who don't espouse these rapturous beliefs). In other words, those with this mindset are literally gambling on *our* collective future—simply based on a *belief*, which *belief* the other half of us find dangerous. More simply put, if one of the 2,100 different gods from 4,200 of the world's different religions does not come "to save us" (or save *you,* because the rest of us are going to hell), then what? It is my greatest desire and sincere hope to have people see both the arrogance and ignorance in this myopic paradigm, because I was raised in (and maintained) this errant mindset for 45 years.]

These timely disruptions afford us *time*. Time to rethink. Time to re-educate. Time to reformat. Time to redistribute; while we have the luxury of having options. Much like tremors and earthquakes, with effective redistribution through minimal disruption, the pressures and stressors are released over time and over a greater area, avoiding larger, more destructive quakes.

Other than a temporary interruption of income to Wall Street and the *one-percenters*, there is literally nothing to lose in this line of thinking. Think *redistribution,* and support it when you see it, if it makes sense to you. But first consider its butterfly effect: the potential *good* and *bad.*

Well thought out redistributive models typically offer universally-beneficial solutions that better address the problems facing not only humankind, but also *all* species on this planet. Our window of opportunity for changing the destructive *status quo* is narrowing every day. Think, act, and thrive—and *help* others to do the same. The body is only as healthy as its components, all the way down to the cellular level.

ABOUT THE AUTHOR

Ronald M. Karren is a single-parent of three terrific individuals, whom he raised over the past decade. Throughout his life, he has engaged in various forms of activism on the local and state levels, and served as an attaché to a senior state senator. In this capacity, he advocated for various parental-rights issues; and was key in repealing compulsory-arbitration laws in healthcare. Recently, his endeavors include bringing ecclesiastical child abuse (and its organized cover-up) to light, enabling him to meet and work with victims and their families worldwide.

Mr. Karren studied Political Science and International Relations, receiving a Bachelors Degree from Brigham Young University. Paying his way through school, he managed at a *Fortune 500* print firm, refurbished and flipped homes, and owned a high-end rod n' reel shop, *Great Basin Fly & Outfitters.* [To remain true to himself and the causes he champions, Mr. Karren feels he must disclose his disappointment in both his alma mater, and more so, its controlling body.]

From 1998 to 2005, he designed and marketed a multimedia educational tool. This venture was vital in enabling him to meet and work with several leaders in a variety of industries. The takeaway from each relationship was integral to his personal and professional development.

In 1999/2000, Mr. Karren worked on a project with Dr. Marc Micozzi at the Thomas Jefferson Institute of Integrative Medicine. With the combined efforts of Dr. C. Everett Koop (former U.S. Surgeon

General), Dr. Deepak Chopra, Dr. Andrew Weil, along with staff from Temple University; their project was a success. Today, many of our U.S. medical schools teach Integrative modalities. From this experience, Mr. Karren gained a greater appreciation for *minimally-invasive* disruption.

In 2002, Mr. Karren was invited by the *Everyday Wealth* team to write and direct an educational production. This noble venture was headed by three of the nation's leading CEOs, including Bill Fields of Walmart. The objective was to instruct the public on *how to get out of debt faster* during the precarious "recovery" years in the wake of 9/11, Enron, and the dot.com crash.

Simultaneously, Mr. Karren was introduced to the Australian banking structure...which changed his life...forever. The rest of the story is found in the book.

Mr. Karren's personal maxim: *Where possible, leave the nouns of this life better than how you found them.*